HOW TO GROW MARIJUANA INDOORS

ENHANCED TECHNIQUES TO BOOST CANNABIS YIELDS

VOLUME 2
BY
CARLOS M. VILLALOBOS

COPYRIGHT

All rights reserved.

DISCLAMER

This book is designed to provide information about selected topics on Cannabis Growing. Every effort was made to create this book as accurate as possible, but no warranty is implied.

The author shall have neither liability nor responsibility to any person or entity concerning any loss or damages arising from the information contained in this book.

The information in the following pages are broadly considered to be truthful and accurate of facts, and such any inattention, use or misuse of the information in question by the reader will render any resulting actions solely under their purview.

The information found in this book is intended for informational purposes only and should thus be considered, universal.

Table of Contents

Introduction..7
Chapter 1
Grow Medium Considerations..........................10
Chapter 2
Low-Stress Training Techniques......................14
Chapter 3
Setting up your growing Area 18
Chapter 4
Deploying Monster Cropping 24
Chapter 5
How to protect against Toxin Air-flow.......................32
Chapter 6
Manifolding AKA Mainlining Step-by-step 36
Chapter 7
Marijuana Ventilation Requirements........................ 48
Chapter 8
Timeline Manipulation Techniques 51
Chapter 9
Defoliation Technique 55
Chapter 10
Topping VS Pinching 64
Chapter 11
Cheap yet Priceless Gadgets you must have..............73
Chapter 12
How to Identify trichomes at Harvesting..................76
ABOUT THE AUTHOR... 82

Introduction

Congratulations on purchusing this book and thank you for doing so. This book is an outstanding beginner's guide to learn how to grow Marijuana indoors.

The subjects of this book are straight forward, thus there are few practical terms mentioned that are wildly used and extremly beneficial to learn.

Each chapter is well detailed to deliver a better understanding to anyone new to these subjects. Ordinary English has been used through this book to avoid misperception; hence no growing experience or any prerequisite is required.

The book will begin explaining what kinds of growing medium are available to you and which ones you should select according to your specific requirements.

Next, you will comprehend the implication of your growing area, and how to create an atmosphere where your Marijuana plants will flourish. Additionally, you will learn what choices you have to keep your plot controlled, and what alternatives you can find on the marketplace. Moreover, you will learn the significance of scent and air-flow toxin regulation for your indoor grows spot or greenhouse.

Likewise, you will learn what choices you have to retain your household feeling hygienic, and your Marijuana plants vigorous. Moreover, you will learn the impact of proper airflow in your growing area, and what choices you have to retain your plants inhalation energetic.

Besides you will also learn why your plants will advance from decent air movement, and what your choices are to achieve decent air movement.

In addition, you will comprehend how and when to flush your plants, how to identify trichomes and their periods, and understand when the flushing process is near completion.

Next, you will learn how to implement Low-Stress Training Techniques, such as screen of green, monster cropping and super cropping.

Next, you will learn how to deploy High-Stress Training Techniques like pinching, topping, defoliation and mainlining. Next, you will learn how to influence yield periods by switching light sequences, and you will comprehend how to implement appropriately both techniques called "Sea of Green" and "12-12 From Seed" for growing Marijuana indoors.

As you can see there are plenty of information to gain from this book and because you are reading this, I would like to congratulate you once again! You have taken the first step to advance yourself on how to grow Marijuana indoors as a Professional cultivator!

There are plenty of contents on this subject on the marketplace, therefore thanks again for picking this one! Every effort was made to ensure the book is riddled with as much valuable data as possible. Please enjoy!

Chapter 1

Grow Medium Considerations

While decide on your growing medium might be one of the easiest decisions you have, selecting your medium itself can be a bit difficult.

The growing medium is where your Marijuana flower will be growing which could be a flexible plastic material, but a fabric pot can do it too.

If both; the soil and the basket are inside hydroponics that is one of the best choices you can have.

There are a small number of opportunities for those horticulturists utilizing soil.

You might try to mature Marijuana in soil jars, plastic pots or fabric made containers.

The drawbacks of a soil or porcelain vessel are that they are heavy even without the medium and they are also the more high-class substitute.

If you are thinking about putting your plants somewhere to be visible, you don't need to spend more cash for this purpose.

While this is how this tool helps, they frequently come in a beautiful fashioned, decent artistic appeal.

Malleable tubs are the economical choice for sure, and they are providing a simple way for horticulturists that won't be putting their plants in a visible place.

When it comes to fabric materials, they are ideal for your plants development mostly since they allow for better airflow to the bottom of your plants.

Hence the greater gamble for an improved flower and more abundant harvest.

Likewise, they are in a more expensive category compared to malleable vessels, but they are robust and rather disposed to rip and wear out.

Regards to hydroponic types of systems, they are rather lesser direct, yet when you are ready to judge on which kind to utilize, the bundle comprises the requirements to start developing your Marijuana flowers.

The aids are that after repetition with hydroponic sorts of systems you don't want to work with it all the time, and eventually they will give you free time too.

Equally, by removing earth you disregard, one more adjustable in your plot, creating smaller chances that your plants will be hurt from illness or similar subjects.

The shortcomings of this are that inclines to be a continued education to nurture your hydroponically system setup, but after a while these classifications can get somewhat costly.

If you are a rookie cultivator, your greatest chance is to nurture traditionally, using water and soil.

There is no considerable dissimilarity in the kind of containers you will find, regardless of your selection, it will most likely be the inexpensive gear you should go with to carry on your indoor grow plot.

Summary:

There are limited pots to select from to your grow spot and all of them have their advantages and disadvantages.

The greatest ranges I endorse in terms of pots are made of fabric material which allows for improved airflow and reach the roots at the bottom of your growing medium.

If you go for the hydroponic system, the modules for nurturing are typically comprised in a bundle once you purchased it.

Chapter 2

Low-Stress Training Techniques

It's time to put the fluff away and learn how to implement the bend and secure technique, the screen of green and super cropping methods.

Before you run away, let me tell you these are perfect for novice growers.

If you're a beginner, you should really master these three techniques before moving on to more advanced high-stress training methods in this book such as popping, man holding, and defoliating.

If you are more like a seasoned grower and need to learn new techniques, go ahead and look through other chapters to advance your knowledge.

Now that's being said, let's dive into the first low-stress training technique called the Bend & Secure Technique.

This is one of the most stimulating ways to train your plants. One of the greatest things you can do is to utalize this technique during the seedling phase, while the stems of the plans are lenient.

After the second set of serrated leaves grows in your plants, gently bend the main stem off to the side without harming it.

Have a plant twist ready in the shape of a hook to lightly secure the top of the stem, and put it away from the middle of the plant.

It is easy, but you need to repeat this procedure with each new stem that goes up towards the center.

The next well known technique you should use to train your flowers is called super cropping.

This technique is frequently used during the vegetative phase, as well before your flowers are moving to the flowering phase.

It is worth to reference that this technique is also used to manage out of control flowers excessively.

In the vegetative phase the Marijuana plant stems will become hard and woody, so you should try to pick a point on the stem where you need it to bend, and squeeze it with your fingers.

Carry on to apply pressure while moving your fingers around it with the stem in between.

After that, continue this process until the branch can easily bend in the direction you need it to.

The process is only going to be completed after the branch stays on the side without restraint.

If you're unintentionally injured the plant in this process, apply duct tape for the fix, and secure the stemming place in a standing position.

If it does happen however, ensure to leave the stem alone to recover.

The next training technique that can be easily applied is called the screen of green.

To accomplish this technique you will need trellis netting.

To apply the screen of green method you will need to start your flowers off with the bend and secure method during the seedling phase.

Next, when you begin the vegetative phase, hang the trellis netting just above your plant canopy.

As your Marijuana plant grows towards the netting, carefully weave the new stems through the holes of the mesh away from the center of the plant.

This technique also has the added help of supporting your plant stems during the flowering phase when your buds can grow chubby and substantial.

These techniques are great for novice growers and I recommend that you utalize them all at the same time and with the same flowers if conceivable.

As you master your skill level, you can acquire and experiment with more advanced training methods.

Chapter 3

Setting up your growing Area

Now it's time to simplify the implication of your growing area to create an atmosphere where your Marijuana plants will flourish, but I will also explain the choices you have to keep your plot controlled.

Similarly with lights there are many alternatives in the marketplace for indoor plot restraint features so let me make things easier for you.

Covering your patch in a grow cabinet, grow tent, or grow room is vastly important for your plants since they demand appropriate light, temperature, airflow, and dampness levels to flourish.

Therefore devouring a controlled plot for your plants will sanction to regulate these aspects and deliver the atmosphere that is ideal for progress.

The first choice available to you is a grow shelter or tent. The benefits of this route far overshadow the drawbacks.

Some of the benefits are that it is the low-priced suppression choice in the marketplace, it is easy to configure, and it's also painless to store while not operated.

Decent tents will have an integral light and sparkly material inside to make the most of the impression of your light, constructed in the ingestion and consume ventilation for the greatest airflow.

Regards to the dense fabric external intersection that comprises the glare of the light in the tent, it also contributes in terms of odour regulations.

Moreover, suitable tents also prone to have a drip plate for more comfortable and better sanitary.

The downsides are that specific shelters can be a bit of a blemish appealing; on the other hand if is in your household, it will appear parallel to a clothing storing stand.

Another limitation is that they only come in very few sizes that may not fit correctly to your growing area as you need them to be.

A next route attainable to the more progressive enthusiastic cultivators is a nurture cupboard. The returns of this are that several of the cupboards accessible on the marketplace now come with high-tech classifications that regulate the airflow, humidity and temperature levels in the closet to improve an ideal growing atmosphere for your Marijuana plants.

Another benefit is that they commonly come fully furnished and assembled; therefore you could begin growing right after you obtain it within a insignificant period.

The flaws are that cupboards are deluxe equally for buying and for delivery as they come clustered upfront.

Likewise, since they are pre-assembled components, you need to be mindful that this purchase will now be an important feature in your home, similarly to your oven or fridge.

Putting it away in a short notice may be a concern. In addition, they have a very commercial look, which may possibly be problematic for those worried about aesthetics in their home.

While a growing shelter can be taken down and concealed fairly rapidly and effortlessly, a grow cupboard is there to terminate.

An additional possibility available to only the most proficient horticulturist out there is a growing cabinet.

The rewards of this are that it delivers sufficiently for a plentiful harvest and allows the formation of an ideal custom atmosphere for your plants to develop.

The drawbacks are that they are expensive to construct, prepare, uphold, and to develop one would mean a substantial quantity of structure and modifications to your household to appropriately set up the ventilation and lighting necessary.

As a consequence, the deviations you create to your household won't be peaceful to converse with the exception that you are eager to feel pain for more construction and overheads yet to come.

A shortcoming to growing cabinets is that not all of them are sufficiently ventilated and preserved flawlessly as you might want them to be.

A danger here that mold and fungus will form on the walls, collaborating the dependability of your home and its resale price.

With that's being said, you might ask: "which choice is best right?" Well, it's subject to a range of things together with skill level, budget, available grow area and estimated harvest to begin with.

Overall extensive declaration yet, the deluxe you'll get for your buck is a grow shelter.

It's low-priced, adaptable and useful for cultivators of all skill level in the same way.

You could find grow shelters all over the web, still, not everything you find is the utmost superiority.

Certain grow tents rip effortlessly while others have elastic bordering that curves without difficulty and don't embrace the heaviness of your light optimally over a specified stage.

Summary:

Your inner plot demands a controlled space to grow in an atmosphere ideal for your Marijuana flower's development.

You have a narrow choice available to you, such as a grow cabinet, grow shelter, grow room, or a grow cupboard.
The most exceptional price for your dollar is a grow shelter.

You could discover these merchandises all over the web, but be apprehensive of shelters made with low-cost fake plastic and light materials.

Chapter 4

Deploying Monster Cropping

Profoundly, monster cropping is just the technique of taking clones from donor plants that already began flowering.

The moniker: monster cropping is came from the potential yields from the technique and the pure quantity of branches that cultivate from placing a clone through the vegetation process over.

The benefits of this technique have been debated for a while since those that do decide to do it are seem to be delighted with the outcomes.

The welfares of monster cropping are numerous. Chiefly, by cloning in the flowering stage no longer required in order to keep a mother plant vegging to harvest yields.

Thus, this frees up some place and gear for other plants. Besides, stressing the donor plants just the right amount should yield the plant if it is done before in the flowering phase, so it has time to pull through. While hypothetically the main benefit of monster cropping, a subsequent plant grows in elegance.

The bush inclines to branch out at all angles creating loads of nodes and therefore bud sites too.

There are certain issues to monster cropping too.

For example taking too many clones from the donor flower can harm the donor plant to the point where growth should sluggish or halt entirely.

As a result, much more trimmings will be desired than cloning through the vegetative phase, as having them to return to vegging is not always good, so the potential accomplishment rate is much slighter.

The major problem that people have experienced with this technique is the amount of time that it takes for the clone to the source and return to veg.

Numerous folks claim that taking clones from a vegging donor and using the screen of green training method will yield the identical outcomes just as monster cropping does.

The splitting is more accidental and robust; however bud site and bud site inferiority differences are slim. Personally, I can see the opinions on both ends.

While the yields can be more considerable with monster cropping, this can be unacceptable to some by the extra time the clones take to route and return to veg.

However, it is exciting to see the monster lags sporadic growth of the branching.

Apart from having a pleasant time while testing with this grow method; I believe the most critical observation you should have for using this cloning technique is in determining whether you have the space for grow spot and lighting to be able to maintain the mother plant.

If you do, this is the best course of action for cloning. Yet if your space and time are limited, give them on stir harvesting a try.

As far as the process to follow; the equipment required for this method does not differ from a regular cloning technique.

While the process for taking the flowering clones from the donor plant it usually's identical, you need to take note of a few things before commencement.

First, ensure that all the gears you are using for the cloning process are spotless and hygienic.

Ensure you have a suitable balance between the number of clones you take from the donor plant without harming the flower and lessening your yields as an outcome.

It's naturally important to make your clones in the 2nd or 3rd week of thriving so the donor plants have enough space to get better from the stress imposed by taking your trimmings.

While in theory, you could still take clippings through the flowering phase.

Take your cuttings from the bottom of the donor plant as replicas taken from here incline to grow sooner than the top half of the flower.

Likewise, don't be frightened to take trimmings that are larger than regular as they often have a better chance of surviving the rooting process.

When the clones are complete and directly placed in water, eliminate all bud sites excluding for the bud side at the top of the trimming.

Be gentle and don't touch the lasting bud site as this could make the clone halt in terms of development.

Put the clones in a vegetative lighting sequence of your choice, like 18 – 6.

Those clones that survived this process will begin to create roots and leaves progressively.

This is when the growing of the clone twitches get more lively, and this will be noticeable.

You should know that this is the right time to start training, using either the screen of green technique or topping if you desire.

Monster cropping clones, harvest certain encouraging results compared to regular twins.

So don't be shocked if your clones begin to grow oddly shaped and deform their leaves at the beginning.

The clones will also be slower to root, so be overly tenacious with them. Repeatedly check if they are still green, as there's still a decent chance they will root.

Clones incline to develop bushes after returned to the vegetative phase, which will affect in sporadic splitting, nodes, and several bud spots.

Typically, the greatest thing you could do is the technique called: the screen of green to support and manage the growth shapes.

Summary:

Monster cropping is the technique of cloning Marijuana during the flowering stage of plant development.

The aids of this technique are that there's no longer need to keep mother flowers, so this opens up space and lighting for other plants.

Additionally, the stress on donor plants should provide extra yields if done appropriately and the resulting clones will grow eagerly with several branches.

The issues are that too many clones taken from a flowering contributor plant should harm the flower and therefore affect your yields.

Also the rooting process and returning the plant to the vegetative phase takes a long time and it is not always effective, therefore several clones need to be measured.

To deploy this technique, follow a regular cloning procedure with some extra notes on the side.

Ensure that you don't take too many trimmings from your donor plants, take your cuttings from the bottom of the contributor, and make clippings a bit larger than average to upsurge odds of existence.

Next, remove all bud sites from the trimming, excluding for the bud site on the top of the replica.

Be optimistic and don't touch the brilliant bud site at the top of the clone, then put the clone under a vegetative lighting sequence.

If possible utilize an 18-6 stage.

Lastly, don't be surprised of clones taken from flowering bushes, take slower to root, crop weird or deformed leaves and develop sporadic after the roots have shaped correctly.

Chapter 5

How to protect against Toxin Air-flow

Now it's time to clarify the significance of scent and air-flow toxin regulation for your indoor grows spot or greenhouse.

Similarly, I will describe the choices you have to retain your household feeling hygienic, and your Marijuana plants vigorous.

The requirement for the right scent and air-flow toxin regulation in your indoor garden will deviate and subject to your budding and how big your plot.

While odor regulation is desirable to accomplish certain flower scents from taking over your home, not every horticulturist need it.

Air-flow toxin regulation otherwise can become problematic for your plants, as well your well-being.

But first let me begin with the wellbeing of your plants. Your cultivating area needs to be healthy to your herbs.

In a nutshell; Garden-fresh, hygienic airborne and air circulation from your cultivation area need to level out the unwelcomed oxygen and build hotness.

Regards to your wellbeing, equally air-flow toxin regulation eases to succeed what is ejected out of your production area and into your household.

This waste product can also catch themselves into your ramparts, creating a matter of anxiety.

What I suggest is a carbon mesh construction, which will fix both of these problems.

A carbon mesh construction will clean the airborne of any fungus and other toxins that can be dangerous to both; you and your plants.

While we on the subject of scent, a carbon mesh construction has the extra gain of scrubbing any odors from the airborne at the top.

Or else, you may decide on an aroma counteracting mediator. But make sure that you don't place the mediator inside or nearby the growing area as it might counterbalance the flavor or your crop.

Aroma counteracting mediator is very valuable and they are inexpensive and extremely dynamic, but they do not sanitize the airborne as a carbon mesh would do.

Carbon filters only pledge to the aromatic scent and counterbalancing it. Any carbon mesh filter is much more respected.

This is because it assists the second resolution of polishing the airborne and counterbalancing the smell, regardless of being the more exclusive choice when it comes to the purchase.

Even so, according to the scope of the grow spot; I still consider you should go with a choice of a carbon mesh.

If you keep your grow area high-pitched spotless, it is not considerably the risk of mold, as it perhaps will pose to your wellbeing and your household.

Mesh filter dimensions vary, but get one that matches the size of your vent distance, and you are going to be just sufficient.

Summary:

Aroma and air-flow toxin regulation are vital to you and your plant's wellbeing.

The carbon mesh construction is your greatest choices irrespective of being the more high-class choice.

Chapter 6

Manifolding AKA Mainlining Step-by-step

If you're a beginner grower, I recommend you first utilize and master low-stress trainings such as screen of green, bend and secure, or super cropping methods.

Regards to these low-stress training methods, once you have mastered them all, you should be able to move on to any high-stress training methods like pinching, topping, defoliation or mainlining.

Mainlining is a training technique that combines the bend and secure method, defoliation and topping strategically.

By defoliating and topping your flower early to branch out from one primary bulge, it produces a manifold for your plants do distribute nutrients and hormones respectively to the highest colas on your plant.

By utilizing this method, it endorses the cultivator to put exertion into training the plant primarily.

Therefore the flower creates a smooth canopy and is much more energizing to control in a reduced space, despite the fact, it still delivers improved than regular harvests.

To apply mainlining on your flower, you will need some essential gear to begin with.

This comprises pruning clippers, a canopy ring, and a horticultural wire.

To apply mainlining on your plants, it needs to be done in phases.

After your Marijuana plants have grown between five and six bulges, it is time to jump on step number one.

You could start later on too, but do not start it in very early stages, as topping your flower too quickly could harm your plant to the point where it may not recover.

Hence after your flower has six bulges, let's implement the first step.

STEP NUMBER 1

Top the flower down to the 3rd bulge. If you haven't topped your Marijuana plant before, this contains eliminating all the plant development above a chosen bulge.

While topping your flower, keep a little bit of the stem residual above the bulge to be linked.

This will ensure you haven't injured the axillary sprouts and will give this area some power and firmness as your flower begins to rely solely on this interconnect to grip it up.

Next, after the topping complete, start to eradicate all the vegetation underneath the interconnect, as well as any sprouts.

You may keep a few leaves in place at this time, as it will endorse quicker budding.

Please confirm all bud sites have been detached. Keep safe both of your new mains at the position equivalent to the ground level.

Still, if it is too early for this and you're concerned about injuring the plant, allow a few days to grow out before securing and bending the new main growth. After you tie them, ensure to utilize tools that won't cut into the new mains, because the rope could cut your plants, while softly covered wiring or green twist ties won't.

Ensure that you get certain airflow on the side with care while tying down your flower, because you don't need to stress it too much at this time.

The aim at this time is to create a strong "T" figure that will be the base for the rest of your flower.

After your two mains have been knotted down, postpone till they crack and point up in the direction of the light, as this will indicate that they have improved from the injury you've imposed.

Next, begin to find new bulges on your mains.

After the new lumps being created, it's time to launch step number two.

STEP NUMBER 2

Here, you need to trace the new nodes on your two mains and top your flower. It is vital to knowledge that you are pointing to create balance in your flower as soon as you are trimming it.

This means you need to cut the same bulge on each of your mains, and if there is more than one bulge, pick the pair of bulges that looks more identical in the distance from the central split in your flower.

This steadiness is critical to the structure of the bush, protecting nutrients and hormones are distributed to the sprouts with the same space and energy, generating even progression and an even canopy.

After you have topped both of your mains, remove more all of the sprouts underneath the bulge you amended. You may pick to remove some or every leaf at this time as well.

At this point, you should have four new mains as a substitute of two. Look after your four new pipes to be equivalent to the ground, directing away from each other. Once this is done, let's move onto step number 3.

STEP NUMBER 3

Regards to this step, repeat step number two.

All you have to do is top your mains for the third time, and this two will fold your pipes even more, generating eight.

To indoor gardeners, I would recommend you to halt at eight mains.

Outdoor growers even in a greenhouse can top up to four or even five more times, generating up to thirty-two mains with each bush.

It's vital to remember that every period you select to cut your flower, you need to do the identical process with every main.

Balancing uniformity are fundamental when mainlining. Let's move onto step number 4

STEP NUMBER 4

This step is voluntary but extremely endorsed for those who are not utilizing the screen of the green in association with mainlining method.

What you can do is buy a tomato ring or canopy disc and discreetly protect your mains to the ring.

The payback here is that your Marijuana plant in the future will create chubby weighty colas.

Equally, it supports the colas far sufficiently because this way it will gain plenty of light from all perspectives.

If you are a notice grower and you only see one or two colas that are developing taller than the others, all you have to do is a moderately super crop it and protect it to the canopy ring to transfer it back in stripe with the rest of your other colas.

STEP NUMBER 5

Respects to this step, keep an eye on the parts you protected with the twist ties.

After the manifold has taken form, it is vital to eliminate the cabling, saving it in place as it can obstruct and harm your plants as your bush expands it.

Similarly, check for any other extents on your flower that you have protected it sufficiently.

STEP NUMBER 6

This step contains substituting your Marijuana plants to the flowering technique and look after the progress.

The weighty lifting of the training procedure is now done, and you need to keep on eye and frequently regulate to retain an even shelter.

After your flower spreads a height of about 17-23 inches high, it's time to make the shift.

If you see any colas rising higher than the others, slowly pull them off on the side till they are in line with the rest, and protect them appropriately.

Consider mainlining after your flower reaches about four or five bulges in the early vegetative phase.

Any faster you proceed doing this; you jeopardize harming your flower beyond recovery.

To anticipate this technique, you need to ensure your flower to this point has been healthy and is growing fast and steadily.

It is an exceptional technique to utilize when growing inside in a reduced space to get the best out of your yield per square foot of your growing area.

If you have never done it, or not done it correctly, you might be sceptical, but here is the thing; agonising the main stem in two into the early phases of plant development neutralizes the plants, incline to harvest a single leading cola.

Continuing to cut the mains at the same intermissions generates a consistently circulated set of colas that completely effortlessly charges nutrients and hormones an equivalent distance from the roots, hence inhibiting the flower from favouring any main stem is priceless.

By confiscating all the sprouts, leading up to your central twigs, it tolerates the bush to emphasize on generating huge colas, full of equal dimensions of germs.

Equally, because of the level of early training on the plant's life, it's now encouraged to improve the whole flowering phase deprived of much courtesy whatsoever.

Summary:

Manifolding or mainlining is a training technique that uses the bend and secure method, topping and the defoliation technique in a way that enhances cola production for an intense harvest.

You will need pruning clippers, canopy ring and plant twist ties to apply it suitably.

Only begin with manifolding after your flower cultivates at least five or six bulges, and top down to the 3rd bulge.

Remove all sprouts and vegetation underneath the bulge you topped previously.

Protect your new mains at a parallel perspective to the ground level.

Begin step two, before your plants have started to nurture toward the light and have few bulges.

Select the same node to top of every mains, ensuring they're an equivalent expanse from the first dominant split in the bush you completed.

Next, eliminate all undergrowth underneath the new bulge splitting and protect your new mains corresponding to the ground level, directing away one-to-one.

Regards to step number three, repeat step number two to generate eight mains instead of four colas.

If you are growing inside, halt at eight colas.

If you are growing outdoors or in a glasshouse, go ahead and endure topping your flower up to four, but no more than five times, generating up to thirty-two mains.

Regards to step number four, protect your growing bush to a plant shelter ring for nourishment, but it's an extra homework.

Regards to step number five, you have to remove any confining secure ties on your bush, or you could eliminate them all carefully.

In conclusion to step number six, you could shift your bush to the flowering phase when it has matured in the middle of 17 and 23 inches from the ground level.

In conclusion, remember if you are in preparation to utilize this method, be confident that your flower is robust, fast-growing and vigorous.

Chapter 7

Marijuana Ventilation Requirements

In this section I will explain the impact of proper airflow in your growing area.

Additionally, I will provide details of the choices you have to retain your plants inhalation energetic.

Besides I will teach you why your plants will advance from decent air movement, and what are your choices to achieve decent air movement.

First of all, it doesn't matter how big your plot is because it's always important to sustain decent airflow to endorse healthy Marijuana plant growth.

Your plant needs a continuous fresh source of carbon dioxide to become lively, and if you are avoiding it, your flower won't be able to advance and eventually die.

Another advantage of decent airflow is that the fresh breeze reinforces your flower's branches, constructing them denser and able to provide a greater harvest at crop. There are limited ways to protect your plant, and one is to allow it to correctly receive the air rotation it needs.

The first technique is to have one or more ventilation in your growing area.

Exactly how many fans you need and their scope will hinge on the extent of your growing area.

The aim here is to see the top of your plant to be whizzing.

So, make sure the fan is not pointed right at your plants to circumvent breeze injury.

The next approach to your growing area has decent air movement is to make sure that you associate an exhaust vent.

This will protect the air is being distributed inside your growing area can outflow when it has been recycled by your plants.

Having a suitable exhaust fan will pull garden-fresh airborne into your growing area to seal the annulled air.

Thus, be certain you verify when buying a fan that it has an identical distance as they consume ventilator in your growing area.

Summary:

Your Marijuana plants need a healthy and steady source of carbon dioxide to continue developing.

So it is important to mount one or more wavering fans in your growing area and make sure that the used air is evading the zone and not overpowering your plants.

Chapter 8

Timeline Manipulation Techniques

In this section I will explain how to influence yield periods by switching light sequences.

The key points of this chapter are to comprehend both techniques called "Sea of Green" and "12-12 From Seed" for growing Marijuana indoors.

I will explain these methods and how to implement them to your indoor gardening appropriately.

In a nutshell, these methods are revolving around manipulating the development stages of the flower and are not technically teaching anything.

As I just revealed, both the 12-12 From Seed and Sea of Green techniques are not training techniques as such, instead, they are planted stage timeline manipulation systems.

Each process is used to false the biological timer of your Marijuana plants, compelling them into the flowering phase of development as soon as possible for faster yield revenues.

When it comes to the 12-12 From Seed method, it comprises growing your plants from seed to crop on a 12-12 light sequence.

What it means in plain English is that you are providing to your Marijuana plants 12 hours of light continuously, and then 12 hours of darkness each day.

Yet, there are a couple of points I want you to be aware.

The concern with this system is that it maneuvers the growth of your flowers, causing such a small crop that it doesn't even make sense to grow in the first place.

Of course, you could still yield in about four months with much superior harvest by solely postponing, after you apply the 12-12 light schedule sequence.

However, the 12-12 sequence being applied from seed, your flower cannot initiate the flowering phase until is at least three weeks on.

Given that your flower has less than 18 hours of light in the course of this stage, doesn't assist your bud, instead it damages it.

Therefore, if you providing your plant with an 18-6 cycle for the first three weeks (about 20), it bears the plant to grow robust enough to give a much healthier and superior yield, while still keeping within range of a four-month harvesting period.

If you're growing in a condensed area and you're concerned that the flower is rising too big, specific elementary training practices can alter this.

The substitute timeline manipulation technique which is known as the Sea of Green, is an additional growing practice comprises the earlier debated light manipulation approach to generate a fast crop revenue with many small colas instead of only one significant cola.

In order to apply the Sea of Green method, numerous cultivators will shift from an 18 to 6 light sequence schedule to a 12 to 12 light sequence schedule when the plants are about 4 to 6 weeks old, dependent on what scope of harvest is their aim, or how much time they have distributed for growing.

Respects to how many small plants you nurture using the Sea of Green technique will be governed by the magnitude of your growing area, and the power of your growing lights.

A good rule for this technique is to go by four and sixteen small plants for every single square meter.

Chapter 9

Defoliation Technique

Now it's time for you to learn how to appropriately defoliate your Marijuana plants.

In summary, you will learn how to teach your plants by using a technique called "defoliating".

Besides, what is the procedure, when you should implement defoliating and how it will improve sophisticated yields for your Marijuana plants.

Before carry on reading this chapter, I would like to remind you that if you're a novice cultivator, I advise you should totally understand and utilize the low-stress systems such as the screen of green, super cropping and the bend and secure methods.

I have already explained these methods previously. Thus, I won't cover those methods here.

Yet, you should only move on with this chapter once you become skilful at low-stress exercise methods such as pinching or topping.

Defoliation is a high-stress Marijuana training technique that encompasses systematically eliminating fan leaves from your plants to develop sophisticated yields.

It's a system that's been argued by expert cultivators on efficiency for an extended stage.

Defoliation can affect a lot of stress for your plants and brutally harm it beyond recovery if it isn't done precisely.

If you are a beginner or in-between grower looking to progress away from low-stress training methods, consider trying the "topping" method first before attempting to utilize the "defoliation" method.

Once you are ready to utilize the defoliation technique, you should begin by eliminating the biggest leaves of your plant, however be extremely watchful not to harm any bud spots at all.

Remove leaves from the bottom first, instead begin with the ones that are not advancing from light irrespectively.

Be vigilant not to confiscate a lot of fan leaves, because it should harm your plants beyond recovery. It will be still dangerous to perceive through this procedure, so please remember this as you gradually defoliate in phases.

Also do not eliminate too many leaves in one session. Initiate with the bottom of the plant and discard only the biggest leaves.

Begin with leaves that are intersecting or near the centre of the plant and are not benefit access to any light, and allow your plant some stage to improve.

Typically at least ten days, but in certain cases should take even double that when it comes to the next stage of eliminating leaves, but it also depends on how fussy your plants are.

Eventually, you have to work your way up the plant in intermissions.

Typically, novice defoliators eliminate too many leaves, so do not make this miscalculation.

Remove less than you think you should to be harmless and do not remove more than about 20% of the leaves at once.

You only need to intend defoliation if you are growing your plants inside. Similarly, if there are preceding concerns with your flower, you need to deal with these matters in advance defoliating your plants.

For illustration, if your leaves are staining or twisting and disappearing, this is not a reason to defoliate your Marijuana plants.

You want to do something about these indications and allow your plant to mend before defoliating them.

Hold up until your flower has at least six bulges and is through the seedling phase before you attempt to defoliate them.

You need to defoliate in stages leading up to bud. Keep the lesser leaves at the top to support your flower engross energy and feed up your sprouts.

If the straining of your flower is acknowledged to be fussy or is now pretty thin in terms of undergrowth, utilizing the defoliation technique is possibly not the right decision.

The defoliation technique only should be utilized above all with your shaggier more strong tensions.

When your flower shifts over to the flowering phase, consider suspending any more high-stress exercise because most of the energy of your bulbs should be engrossed on generating large sprouts in the progress of this stage.

Normally, you can carry on exhausting low-stress methods through this stage.

As a reminder, you could still defoliate through the flowering phase, but I wouldn't recommend it if you are new to utilizing this method.

After completing this technique through the vegetative phase, you should try it in the flowering phase, but be very cautious.

Equally, you only need to plan the defoliation technique if you have: good enough lights, your bush has been fit and fast-rising, your flower has been robust in its entire lifecycle, and the leaves are resting on top of each other or forming glooms over the plant sprouts.

To defoliate in the course of the flowering phase, first eliminate every leaf that is forming shadows above your main sprouts.

You should try to aim only the larger leaves but stand by the similar elimination instructions as you did through the vegetative phase. Keep the slight leaves, as your bush will gain from them later. Your objective over this period is to expose lots of sprouts to light as feasible.

If you thinking about why you should get rid of the leaves, let me explain.

Your Marijuana wants to survive and it wants to generate energy, and energy is generated from their leaves.

Yet, if you go ahead with the technique of defoliation correctly, you are not eliminating all the leaves, preferably just the big ones that aren't benefiting from the light provided in any case.

If you are growing indoors, your flowers are in a measured atmosphere and do not necessitate its leaves as it would in the open.

Outside, your plant would profit from these leaves to cover from a range of ecological vulnerabilities.

Thus, the concept is that your indoor plants will benefit from defoliation for a variety of intentions.

For illustration, a smaller quantity of leaves means extra light will enter the sprouts through the flowering phase, causing advanced harvests.

Your flower will similarly have fewer additions to take care of, distracting more of its energy and effort to the sprouts, and this result in quicker growth and superior harvests.

Lastly, more leaves usually mean higher dampness intensities.

This can be problematic to your flower as it can generate mold and develop an inhabitable surrounding for the plant.

Therefore appropriate defoliation of your Marijuana plant will result in a superior harvest, but it will similarly endorse a more parallel development in your flower.

This will develop a beautiful flat sunshade that will enhance your inside lights.

Summary:

Remember that you should only consider the defoliation technique if you have become skilled at all other low-stress methods and wish to investigate and progress your education.

Defoliation means that you are eliminating the biggest leaves and do not eradicate a lot of them at one go.

You need to be proceeding in stages, sanctioning at least ten, but in certain cases even twenty days between each stage for your plants to repair.

After you begin with the defoliation technique, you should start with the bottom of the plants.

Do not remove more than 20% of leaves at each stage. Leaves that are out of sight or concealed, need to be cut off primarily.

Do not defoliate your plants, unless you are growing indoors.

Do not defoliate your plants, unless they are healthy and robust, rising fast, and having strong tensions.

You might go ahead and begin the defoliating technique in the vegetative phase, after your bush has at least five or six bulges and is not in the seedling phase.

If you decide on continuing defoliating while in the flowering phase, confirm your light is adequate, and your flower is vigorous, reliable and acceptable to survive.

Over the period of the flowering phase, remove all leaves that are forming a shadow above your main sprouts.

Aim only the larger leaves or any overlying leaves.

Keep the lesser leaves, since your Marijuana plant will still yield from these in the future.

Chapter 10

Topping VS Pinching

Now let me explain the difference between some of the most well-known high-stress training techniques called "pinching" and "topping".

I will describe how to apply each method, when you should start utilizing these methods, and what reactions your plants will have.

As with any other high-stress training techniques if you are a novice cultivator, I suggest you first understand the low-pressure training methods like the screen of green, super cropping and bend & secure.

Once you mastered the low-pressure preparation techniques, only then you should go ahead and begin learning high-stress training practices such as pinching, topping, defoliation or mainlining.

First let me begin with a technique known as topping. One of the most famous plant training system called topping is where you deliberately eliminate the top development of the main branch, so the flower as a whole grows more parallel similarly to a Christmas tree but vertically.

This system also has other benefits of generating two key stems as a substitute instead of one.

To top your plants, you need to trace the critical stalk and separate the most present development collection on it.

Inspect the stem to the neighbouring cross that has fan leaves. This interconnect is named a bulge.

At this bulge, you will see two signs of progress which are named axillary sprouts.

This is the place where you are successful in being topping your Marijuana plants, and the axillary germs will progress to develop the new main stalks on your plants.

After topping the plants, do not try to cut too near to the bulge, instead slightly a few centimetres above the cross.

This will ensure you have not injured the sprout sites in the topping procedure and allow certain strengthening to the zone as your plants grow large and sturdy. It's vital not to top your plants too soon, but if you go ahead with it, this should harm your plants to the point where they may not make any progress.

As a common rule, don't anticipate topping till your plants have at least four bulges in the course of its vegetative phase of development.

If you're uncertain, think through how much of the flower you're eliminating.

If you were to split your flower up into units, you would be eradicating one fifth of the flower, or close to seven.

Logically, the lesser the fraction of the total flower you are eliminating, the more expected it is to recuperate.

When you've topped it, keep as is for a few weeks to improve before allowing any other high-stress training technique.

By eliminating the new development down to the neighbouring bulge, you are permitting light to enter the axillary sprouts as it would never have been able to before.

Your plant knows this and begins to focus its liveliness on generating new main stalks that will arise from these places.

You need to see instantly after topping your flower that the associates at the bulge have become inflated to provision the development spurt that is impending.

This obsession is how you know that the energy is being side-tracked to the zone, and you've accomplished the procedure appropriately.

This technique will work to decrease the tallness of your plants, making a table top like construction as an alternative to a Christmas tree shape.

This is particularly beneficial for indoor growing operations.

The technique will generate two consistently dispersed main colas as a substitute of one, which will benefit your harvests as your plants begin to flower and have sufficient space to engross light rundown of distressing about being outshined.

Regards to the technique known as pinching, it is similar to topping, yet somewhat diverse. Hence it has slightly different outcomes too.

Similarly to topping, you have to trace the main stem at the most current development.

As an alternative of cutting a few centimetres overhead the neighbouring bulge like with topping, when it comes to pinching it comprises shredding or shaving the top of the new development without harming the stalk.

After shaving off the top development, remove about three third of it to get the best grades possible.

The faster you consider endeavouring to tweak your plants is in the duration of the vegetative phase of development after your plants have at least four bulges.

When it comes to pinching, it is far less aggressive than topping.

Thus, plants are much more rapid to recuperate if they realize what happened whatsoever.

The subsequent result is that your plants will nurture in the middle of three colas, yet it is far less systematized than the topping method.

If you chose to pinch your flower later in the development through the vegetative phase, this will have side effects in the lower stalks on the flower getting up to generate a table top, comparable to a production.

If you thinking about why you would anticipate applying topping if pinching is less aggressive and delivers more buds, then let me provide an answer.

Let's begin with the fact that topping provides more benefits to your flower at the stage of the flowering phase, allowing light to enter the potential areas with grander ease for chubbier sprouts.

Besides, if pinching is not done inaccurately, your plants will end up with two or maybe three buds as a replacement for four.

This is somewhat achievable with better precision by just topping your flower two times.

When it comes to topping, it does have a slow-moving development on your plant; therefore if you do this about two times, it might not be your most significant choice if you want a fast crop.

It is also likely to tweak your plants before topping them for greater harvests, but I recommend you to try these methods out individually within a couple of intervals before undertaking them together on the same plants.

If you want the biggest harvest possible, I advise applying low-stress training methods such as the screen of green, bend and secure or super cropping approaches in correspondence with pinching and topping.

If your plants are rising too big, you might scratch them a little using the topping technique if it's essential, yet remember that you'll be wasting the development stage.

Hence the vegetation phases will possible needs to be sustained.

In conclusion, it's vital not to pinch or top your plants in the course of the flowering stage as this harms your plants, while it requires exclusive attention to generate chubby sprouts, instead of mending themselves.

Summary:

The technique called plant topping is nothing but eliminating the most current development from the top of the plant to generate dual colas in a place of one.

After your flower has developed about four to five bulges, trim off the top development of the flower just above the central bulge.

If you go ahead and top your plant too early, it is likely that it won't make any progress whatsoever.

Regards to the technique of pinching, it won't damage the stalk at all; hence it is less destructive compared to topping.

To pinch your flower correctly, you need to remove three third of the development at the top of your plant deprived of disturbing the stem even slightly.

The correct stage for pinching is once it has at least four bulges.

You can utilize these methods in cooperation at the equal interval, and in correspondence with low-stress training techniques, yet, you should only begin using these methods once your plants have reached the flowering stage.

Chapter 11

Cheap yet Priceless Gadgets you must have

Moving on, let me give you some tips on a few pieces of tools that will be extremely beneficial to your growing area.

Some of those important tools include an automatic timer and a thermometer.

The benefit of a thermometer is that it preserves you efficient on the atmosphere in your growing area. In a nutshell, it allows you to regulate and control your atmosphere and grow area.

If there is something better then a thermometer is known as a "thermo hygrometer".

This gadget will be intelligent enough to tell you both temperature and humidity levels in your growing area, and it would only cost a little more than a thermometer would.

Lacking this small piece of gear, there is a lot of deduction connected to these variables that might delay the development of your Marijuana plants.

It would be slightly less cash if you go ahead and purchase it, and let me tell you, it is worth considering it.

The next equipment that will be helpful to your plants and will save you time and irritation is an involuntary clock for your grow lighting.

This gear will definitely help you as you will have to physically turn on and off your light each day at the exact same time.

The stages of lights your plant requires day-to-day links right to its phase of development, and if you unintentionally miss even a day, it may possibly modify the undergrowth and thriving stages of your plants development.

A minor asset, but this kit will protect you and save you time and anxiety in the same time.

Another tool that you will require is either a digital microscope or a Jeweler's loupe. This will be extremely helpful in terms of timing your harvest, which I will explain in more detail in the next chapter.

Summary:

An automatic clock and a thermo hygrometer are straightforward requirements that are inexpensive and valued highly for your venture.

Regards to the atmosphere of your growing area, a thermo hygrometer will always inform you.

While a lighting clock will help you so your Marijuana plant gets the light it desires for each phase of its development.

Chapter 12

How to Identify trichomes at Harvesting

While everyone knows that Marijuana plant require watering, most people unaware of some great tricks they could use, or worse unsure when to water plants correctly.

Personally learned it in the hard way, but I will save that story for another time.

Watering is one thing but when it comes to harvesting, most novice growers either do it too early or worse, too late.

Now that you made it to this chapter, let me explain how and when to flush your plants.

Moreover, I will explain how to identify trichomes and their periods and understand when the flushing process is near completion.

Within a month or two, your buds should be looking nice and fat, ready for harvesting. If white hairs on your buds are beginning to curl, darken or both at the same time, it is the first sign that your plants are getting close to harvest.

The most significant rule here is to be persistent. Many people harvest too early and lose out on yields and potency for their buds.

You'll possibly have no choice but to wait a few weeks longer than you expect for the greatest results.

An excellent benchmark for most strains is when half to three-quarters of the white hairs on your buds have curled or darkened.

After at least half of the white hairs have curled, it's now time to utilize the microscope or jeweler's loupe.

You will see on your buds that there will be little clear trichomes, looks like mushrooms, as cannabinoid levels rise in the bud when these trichomes begin to get cloudy and white.

After an extended period of time, they can even get an amber color.

It's worth noting at this point that not all strains have their way to darken.

This rule should be used with caution and keep the microscope handy to examine your buds regularly.

The higher the number of cloudy trichomes you have on your bud, the higher the concentration of cannabinoids like THC and CBD, and therefore the more potent the buds will become.

The effects of Marijuana on individuals are varying. Many cultivators subjectively believe that harvest times have a significant impression on the resulting psychological effects of the drug, and as a result you want to know precisely when you should start flushing your plants as well.

The general thoughts around harvest times and its resulting psychological effects are this.

If you're looking for stimulating, energetic and more potent high with a less sedative effect, begin flushing when the trichomes are cloudy.

If you're looking for a more couch lock high or intense body buzz, wait for many of the trichomes to start turning amber before flushing.

If you're looking for a combination of these two effects, begin flushing around half the milky trichomes, once have turned amber in color.

Watering your flowers means that you're no longer giving your plants nutrients, and you're spraying them in the soil of any remaining nutrients, before harvest.

While if you're using a nutrient-rich soil or super soil, there's no need to water your plants as you've not been feeding them with chemical nutrients.

To clean your plants, take care of them the way you would typically with one exception. Stop giving them nutrients of any kind.

This step is necessary for the smell of taste and smoothness of your buds.

For all of the nutrients to flush from both the soil and your plants are takes typically between seven and fourteen days.

If it's your first time growing Marijuana and you're producing multiple flowers of the same strand, a valuable option is to start watering at different times.

It is helpful because you could test different harvesting periods, and determine which one is best for you so that you can apply it with your next harvest.

Make sure you look out for the plant to start yellowing after you've started flushing. Sometimes flowers can turn yellow overnight.

It's normal for the larger fan leaves of your plant to turn yellow, but make sure that you harvest your buds before the sugar leaves begin to yellow.

Sugar leaves are those leaves embedded in the buds.

Summary:

Ensure that you are persistent and water your plants at the right time.

A decent benchmark is when 1/2 to 3/4 of the white hairs have begun to either curl or darkens, and don't forget that not all strains darken in color.

Use a digital microscope or jeweler's loupe to look at the mushroom looking trichomes to judge more precisely whether the buds are set for harvest.

The higher amount of cloudy trichomes means more cannabinoids like THC and CBD.

While the trichomes get darker and amber in color, what this means is that the buds are more sticky, and typically results in more sedative effects on the body when consumed.

When you've pinned the right time for harvest, begin flushing your plants for seven to fourteen days, by not feeding them their nutrient formulas.

After you see the fan leaves at your plants begin to yellow, it is time to harvest your plant.

ABOUT THE AUTHOR

Carlos Martinez Villalobos was born in Guadalajara, Mexico in 1972.

He has received his Diploma at the Universidad de Guadalajara from Pharmacy and Materials Sciences, where he also researched and wrote his first book on Chemistry in 1996.

In 2010, Carlos has moved to Albuquerque, New Mexico, where he got introduced to the fast-growing Medical Cannabis Industry.

His new Journey has begun in 2014 by helping people to teach how to grow Medical Marijuana Outdoors to fight against cancer.

Carlos continues to research on cannabis cultivation, helping patients with insomnia, anxiety and other pain reliefs.

— JUST ANOTHER —
DETOUR

A Practical Guide for Moving through
Painful Moments to Your Next Win!

DR. MIANDA CARR

LUMINARE PRESS
WWW.LUMINAREPRESS.COM

Printed in the United States of America

Cover Design: Melissa K. Thomas

Luminare Press
442 Charnelton St.
Eugene, OR 97401
www.luminarepress.com

LCCN: 2019941767
ISBN: 978-1-64388-129-4

This book is dedicated to my precious daughter, Lily.

I pray you always remain fearless, confident, self-aware, kind, and, best of all, your own version of God's little warrior princess.

CONTENTS

Introduction 1

Chapter 1

Feel the Pain
You Have Permission to Hurt 5

Chapter 2

Find a Different Set of Lenses
Your Pain Is Real, but It Is Not Unrivaled 17

Chapter 3

Face Your Loss
and Count the Cost! 29

Chapter 4

Focus on What You Have Left
There's More There Than You Know 41

Chapter 5

Follow Wisdom's Lead
Rebuild or Start Anew? 51

Chapter 6

Find Your Win
and Celebrate Your Survival! 61

Chapter 7

The "D" Word
A Brief Commentary on Battling Depression . . . 70

INTRODUCTION

According to an old Greek philosopher, "the only constant in life is change." I would add that another irrefutable constant is no matter who you are, painful times in life are inevitable. The circumstances and severity of the pain and crises we experience may vary from person to person and from season to season, but I've discovered the path we're all on will at some point lead us to a rocky, thorny place we were dreading or, worse yet, never expecting. That's not to say that there aren't many days filled with joy, peace, and contentment, but we are not doing ourselves any favors if we choose to deny that there will also be times when we suffer pain, sadness, grief, loss, and unanticipated setbacks. For those of us in the Christian faith, we spend a great deal of time reading about the complicated and often tumultuous lives of biblical heroes, teachers, and prophets, and yet we so often feel confused, abandoned, and disillusioned in our own faith when life takes serious downward spins.

In my mid-thirties, I was hit with this dilemma. By this time, I had earned a notable academic performance record, received my medical school degree, and successfully completed a residency program in my chosen specialty of obstetrics and gynecology. I had relocated my Midwestern roots to new, fertile soil out west and was looking forward to the next phase of my life with a great deal of optimism and excitement. The initial years in this new season just about met my every expectation, and I had no doubt I was every bit the champion in Christ that I always believed myself to be.

Little did I know, the next phase of my life would not be lived out to the familiar tune of a champion. I found myself being hit by a succession of challenging events, one after another, for about seven years. From a professional lawsuit to another marriage and second divorce, single parenting, health challenges, career burnout, and, ultimately, depression, I found myself questioning if I would ever find my way out of that dark valley of pain and crisis.

As you are reading these words, what I've described of my experiences during those years probably sounds familiar to you. In fact, you are the reason why I decided to write this book with such relatability and transparency. You see, when I finally found my way around each of these obstacles and out of the pitfalls set on my path, I realized that I had spent nearly a decade wandering around a wilderness for which I had no strategy and little preparation. When the pain, heartache, and disappointments ran deep enough to drive a stake through my once-impenetrable foundation of religious faith and inner strength, I felt helpless, alone, and uncertain about the future. These may have been among the worst times of my life to date, but I don't believe they were without great purpose. When I emerged, this guidebook was born.

I learned many important truths on that journey, and the most valuable of all is that *we truly can convert just about every painful situation we face into a life win.* The path that leads us from pain to healing is winding, unlevel, and dimly lit if there's any real light or clarity at all at the start of the journey. This is further complicated by the fact that no two paths are exactly alike, varying from person to person and from crisis to crisis, yet we don't have to stumble around in the darkness passively waiting for the hurt, regret, and bitterness to fade away. We can hold fast to the faith that grounds us *and* equip ourselves with tools we can use to process our pain with the intention of uncovering our own victories, great and small. The chapters in this guidebook help us navigate through the steps we can take to help push through the fog. We may not avoid experiencing some painful times in this life, but *we can survive* them and *we can* take practical steps to find our *win*!

Find Your Win

Follow Wisdom's Lead

Focus on What You Have Left

Face Your Loss

Find a Different Set of Lenses

Feel the Pain

CHAPTER 1

Feel the Pain
You Have Permission to Hurt

"We must embrace pain and burn it as fuel for our journey."

—Kenji Miyazawa, Japanese Poet

"Don't worry." "Don't let that bother you too much." "You're much stronger than that." "I know you'll be fine." "You have so much to be grateful for." "There are certainly many people out there who have it a lot worse." "Your troubles won't last always!"

Do any of these sound familiar to you? I bet they do! These and other familiar words of encouragement are commonly offered in a sincere attempt to comfort and reassure another going through difficult times. Whether it's a parent to a child, pastor to a parishioner, doctor to a patient, or friend to a confidant, it appears to be in our human nature, an instinctive reflex, to want to help those who are hurting to

JUST ANOTHER DETOUR   5

push past their pain, worries, anxieties, and fears, straight to the goal line of victory. The intention is good, but here is something to consider. Could a sincere effort to provide comfort at times be misplaced?

I believe that in the right context, any of these life-affirming statements can be comforting for those who are hurting, and I do not discount that. However, envision for a moment that you find yourself suspended thirty thousand feet in the air on an airplane that loses engine power, and the cabin loses pressure. Obviously, for anyone other than an experienced skydiver with a parachute in hand, this would be a terrifying experiencing to say the least, no matter how brief the scare. Now imagine as you grip your armrest paralyzed with fear, heart pounding, pulse racing, making every attempt to pull that oxygen mask down and over your face, the person sitting next to you leans over and says with a sincere tone and empathetic smile, "Don't worry … don't cry … I know you're stronger than that … I'm sure someone, somewhere has it even worse than you right now!" How misplaced and, dare I say, inappropriate would that be in that time of crisis? So many times we offer or are offered the same sincere yet poorly timed sentiments in times of crisis. Though we may not be moving about in a sixty-ton aircraft, threatening to hurtle itself to the earth, often life can feel that way for us when we are experiencing personal crises, challenges, losses, and grave disappointments!

The first lesson here is that in painful times of crisis, grief, and trauma, it is okay to stop and allow yourself to feel the hurt, the pain, and the fear! In order to achieve our healing, it is often imperative to dig our heels in for a moment and acknowledge the despair and pain that we feel. No matter the trauma we suffer, whether it is physical, emotional, financial, or relational, whether public or private, we must take the time we need to withdraw from our routines, turn our attention inward, and allow ourselves to connect with what is going on deep inside of ourselves. Now this may look different to different people. For example, a wealthy person who has suffered an unexpected heartbreak or other personal loss can afford to drop everything to retreat to a private island to grieve. On the other hand, for most of us, our break from the routine may have to be far more practical, for in the real world, it is not an option to drop everything and run off to a remote part of the earth. Yet, it is vital that we find some way to tap into the space beyond the world around us with all of its expectations, deadlines, and pressures, and just … feel.

Help! I'm Hurting!

Now I know this may not seem like a deep or novel concept, but let me show you how important it is that I started off with this seemingly obvious or intuitive directive for our first step on this journey to feel the pain of hurt. For the person who has suffered a fall and broken bone, there is likely no reason to remind them to stop for a moment and recognize the excruciating pain they feel in the moment. I admit I have never experienced a physical trauma as serious as a broken arm or leg (and pray that I won't ever have to!), but I have spent enough time around urgent care facilities and emergency rooms to know that a person in this much physical pain does not need to be told by the family, nurse, or doctor that serious pain is their current reality—they are well aware!

Here's an important question we should ask ourselves—what makes the most critical impact on a person's well-being? Is it physical or emotional hurt? It's an interesting thought, right? Well, I would argue that negative or painful emotional experiences may be equally or in some cases more lasting and traumatic than the physical or sensory pain we feel in response to injury.

Let's revisit that poor person we left in the ER with the broken limb a moment ago. Regardless of how the injury occurred, we can safely say that the initial step in the chain of events that will lead to relief and healing is recognizing that the injury has occurred in the first place. Okay, that's a nice way of saying there was probably serious hollering and screaming going on as the bone broke. Perhaps even cries for help, drawing the attention and aide of witnesses and those nearby. Now we have all probably seen that tough person suffering from terrible pain who is trying their best to "conceal without the squeal." We see this often in professional sports. All it takes is one camera close-up on the grimacing face of the strong, professional athlete with their leg twisted up, and there is no mistaking their attempt at silence for an agony that demands immediate medical attention!

After the gravity of the situation has been assessed, the injured party is whisked away to the nearest hospital or urgent care for a thorough evaluation by trained medical personnel. Further management may include care for an open wound and control of bleeding, stabilization of the limb, x-rays, and, if no surgery is required, application of a cast or splint. After the necessary process of healing, the once-fractured bone is not only intact but functional again. Success, right? Wait, in discussing our care for the injured party, we skipped *one of the most important steps*, especially from the perspective of the injured party. Yes, we carefully addressed the problem of the broken bone, but *have we addressed the excruciating pain*? You can bet that on arrival to the ER, the pain medication that he or she was given to relieve the acute pain provided the calm and comfort needed to allow proper care to continue.

The Danger in Denying Your Pain

In response to the above scenario, we can say with confidence that there was never a question whether the injured party should stop to recognize that there had been an important compromise in their health and well-being, nor did it seem unnecessary to address both the pain and the physical injury. I submit that the emotional wounds of disappointment, failure, loss, rejection, or assault that leave our hearts, souls, and dreams lacerated or broken should not be treated with any less significance or urgency. In fact, if you think about it, the physical pain we can experience, especially severe pain, will most often motivate us or our loved ones to seek a life-saving remedy quickly, whereas the burden of sorrow is often carried in silence for far too long. This can lead to depression, anger, despair, and the absence of any real life.

I can attest to the real dangers of trying to move quickly and quietly from hurt to healing without properly addressing the pain. During my mid-thirties, after a whirlwind courtship and engagement of about six months, I was embarking on my second marriage with a spirit of great excitement and renewal. In fact, I felt successful and fulfilled in almost every arena of my life: professional, financial, social, and spiritual. I had reached a time when I was again open to the idea of a long-term, committed relationship. You see, for several years following my first marriage and divorce many years prior, I carried an almost suffocating load of guilt for deciding to marry my first spouse in the headstrong folly of my youth. The challenging years spent surviving a tough medical residency program were further complicated by my difficult decision to initiate separation and divorce in that short time. The painful truth that neither my heart nor my soul was truly committed to that union became too real to ignore. The toll these years took became evident in my tremendous weight loss and social withdrawal. In hindsight, it was clear that letting go was the only right and honest thing to do. However, knowing that I had hurt a kind and innocent person, as well as believing erroneously that I had failed my family, my friends, and my faith, all but destroyed my peace, joy, and any expectation of ever having the kind of love and marriage I had dreamed of for as long as I could remember.

By the time I reached my mid-thirties, I had processed and released the guilt and heartbreak I caused and suffered over the years, and I was in a much better place. Well, that is until I became painfully aware of my age, my singleness, and the familiar biological clock ticking away! As it happens, I met the man who would become (so I thought) my redemption, my "do over," and my natural and spiritual partner in family and ministry. Providence was the only explanation I had for this unforeseen and unexpected opportunity for a second chance at love, marriage, and destiny with another successful and spiritually minded person.

As I mentioned, after a brief but chaste period of dating and engagement, followed by a most memorable and picturesque destination wedding, we set out on a journey that was anything but what I had expected. We were blessed to conceive within the first few months of marriage, as was our hope. Unfortunately, the birth of what would be my greatest disappointment arrived not long after my little bundle of joy. My marriage of promise and second chances ended abruptly, just like that.

It was not just my marriage that ended unexpectedly. Hope ended. Faith began to fade away. Disillusionment was all that remained. With a little one in tow, a growing and demanding profession, a career-defining board examination on the horizon, the professional lawsuit I was fighting, and a separate, silent battle with undiagnosed postpartum depression, I carried on, empty and exhausted but determined, as if the proverbial rug had not been pulled out from under me. In the fog of sleep deprivation, perpetual sadness, and mounting responsibilities, I learned how to keep up the appearance of superwoman by day while wrestling with deep depression. At my lowest point, I even wondered if a life of pain, hardship, and shattered dreams was one worth living.

Eyes Wide Shut

Looking back, I'm most troubled by my inability to confront the turmoil and upheaval in my mind, soul, and spirit. It is true that often our personal battles must be fought and won from within before we can reach out for the support of the others. However, we need to recognize those times when this is not the highest truth for us. In my case, I failed myself on not just one but two fronts. I not only hid my pain and struggle to stay afloat from everyone around me, but what's worse, I chose to avoid my own reality in my quiet hours with myself. I suppose I reasoned that the charge I'd been given years ago to care for others as a physician, along with this new, weighty responsibility as a divorced mother, took precedence over my own heartache. The lights went off for me, and I felt like I was just existing to survive the darkness. I still carried the weight of being the light for many patients during the day and for my daughter at night.

As you're reading this, perhaps you find yourself in a dark place much like this. You may not be facing grave illness or some other threat to your physical well-being, but you know you have been surviving in a "valley of the shadow of the death." This valley where so many of us find ourselves at one point or another does not necessarily represent a physical death but rather the death of our dreams, the death of our love relationships, the death of our career aspirations, and, yes, what looks like the death of our faith. I know that can be tough to admit, especially if you were raised in a strong religious environment as I was. Those of us who have survived this valley and lived to tell about it have found that the fragments of our faith will survive and be recovered when the smoke clears from the valley floor.

As I write this book from the other side of this dark time in my thirties, I can say that I fully embrace the notion that a journey through one of these deep valleys of pain cannot be avoided. How I wish someone, anyone, would have told me that! Oh sure, I had heard others along the way testify about overcoming trials, hardships, and battles, and I had faced and triumphed over personal, spiritual, and academic roadblocks of my own. However, I don't recall any adult or religious leader I knew when I was growing up being transparent about their own encounter with their *valley of the shadow of death*—the one that strips you of just about everything you once knew to be true about life, success, and winning and that forces you to redefine your relationship with yourself, your support network of friends and family, and your God. With all the diplomas, plaques, and awards I earned through the years, I did not feel prepared for the tumble into this deep hollow that swallowed up more than just my vision board. It completely engulfed my heart, my mind, and my soul.

These valley experiences are never unique, though in these times, we feel isolated and alone. I have learned that most people take some version of this painful journey, and what's worse, there is no way for our intelligence or experiential GPS to assist us in avoiding it. Otherwise, we all would! We don't know what decade we will be in when we have to trudge through this valley or what carefully laid life plans will be downright interrupted. We *can* be sure that this valley is not designed to bring about the death of our dreams or our destiny. The pressure applied, and the pain and loss we survive in these dark ravines, can make us tougher, stronger agents of great purpose.

Taking the First Step

Here is the dilemma many of us face. We expect that our faith will move us out of these valleys expediently or, as I believed in great error, ensure we avoid them altogether. Neither is necessarily true. We will have pain in this life. The pain will vary in severity and intensity. There will be times we heal and bounce back quickly, and there will be times that we find it nearly impossible to recover. God is faithful and will not abandon us in the valley, but we may not emerge overnight.

As part of the process of healing and growth, there is a series of practical steps I believe we can take in being intentional about moving toward victory that are perfect companions to our prayer and knowledge of the Word.

The initial step is identifying the painful event that led us to the valley in the first place. Attempts to ignore the throbbing pain, maintain a façade of invincibility, or disassociate altogether from the trauma (all of which I was guilty) will only prolong our time spent in emotional limbo without making real progress toward the healing and destiny awaiting us. Even worse, we can find ourselves caught in a web of depression, self-medication with mood-altering substances, and isolation, all leading to the death of the hopes and dreams we are trying hard to preserve. This first chapter is a challenge to be brave enough to meet the disappointment, personal failure, injustice, betrayal, and heartbreak head on. *This is not a failure of faith but an acknowledgment of our need for help and healing!* The Bible teaches us in Romans 4:17 that God uses His words of faith and authority to call things that are not as though they are—not to call things that are as though they are not! **Failing to acknowledge our pain is not a demonstration of our great and unwavering faith but a harmful practice that causes us to linger far too long in our valleys.** When I ran out of steam trying to maintain life at a challenging pace without properly acknowledging how deeply wounded I was, I found myself right back at this first step, confronting the pain within.

Everyone will confront their most painful times of crisis or loss differently, but the method is not nearly as important as the willingness to be vulnerable. Some prefer to journal, some cry it out, some seek the comfort of trusted friends or loved ones, and some move directly to therapy. *Whatever it takes, the goal is to get to the emergency room, get some pain relief, and get on with the healing.* I believe our journeys through the valley of darkness can be shortened, or at least less arduous and wearying, if we will start by honestly locating where we are—in other words, feeling that very pain we are trying to avoid or deny. Looking back, I regret that I didn't do this sooner, but I take such great comfort in the lessons I learned that I can now pass on to help ease your journey through hardship to wholeness.

Taking a Closer Look

"The Lord is close to the brokenhearted and saves those who are crushed in spirit."

—Psalms 34:18 (New International Version)

If this chapter resonated with you, you are the reason that I needed to write this book. Now, let's take that first step together.

- Is there pain or hurt in your life that you need to acknowledge?

- What factors or beliefs have kept you from doing so?

Find Your Win ●

Follow Wisdom's Lead ●

Focus on What You Have Left ●

Face Your Loss ●

Find a Different Set of Lenses

Feel the Pain ●

CHAPTER 2

Find a Different Set of Lenses
Your Pain Is Real, but
It Is Not Unrivaled

"To know pain is human. To need is human. And no amount of money, influence, resources, or sheer determination will change our physical, emotional, and spiritual dependence on others."

—Brené Brown, Author and Research Professor

If the words in this book were meant for you, the powerful and simple truth of acknowledging pain and hurt has likely hit you harder than you expected. I know—I've been there. Once I was able to face my pain and disappointment, instead of carefully tiptoeing around the shards of shattered dreams along my path to avoid being cut, I set out on the best journey of my life. *A journey that started with a series of painful and embarrassing events ultimately positioned me for some of my greatest personal victories.* However, to move beyond the darkest depths of our valley moments to those places of light, hope, and destiny, we have to find the courage to walk through, not around, our pain. We must be intentional about the steps we take so that we can safely land on higher plains emotionally, physically, financially, relationally, and spiritually. We must not allow ourselves to remain stuck in that place of hurt and disappointment.

Jumping Off the Replay Reel

In today's fast-paced and technology-driven society where information can travel around the globe in an instant, I think about how awful it must be for celebrities, politicians, and others with public personas to have their private failures and misfortunes broadcast via news outlets and social media without delay. Most of us take this level of intrusion and public humiliation for granted, considering it to be "the price of fame." Some of us have been guilty of helping to cultivate the infamous grapevine, repeating salacious and often hurtful gossip about others we don't know or perhaps may have even met. I suppose that's in part because we feel safe from suffering that type of embarrassing exposure and criticism, living our lives outside the limelight.

Even the most private or socially isolated among us can be vulnerable to having painful experiences and personal failures set in replay mode, over and over. We may never know what it's like to wake up and discover our latest personal failure or life crisis trending on the internet or competing for headlines in the daily newsfeed, but the internal replay reel that we take with us everywhere we go can weigh us down and keep us from real forward progress. By reliving painful events in our minds, we can become stuck in what should be only momentary downswings. This creates a vicious cycle, much like a car spinning its tires in a slick snow bank or deep puddle of mud, working to dig a deeper ditch of despair, depression, and self-pity. *In these cases, the pain has been acknowledged but never processed, causing unproductive mental and emotional "tire spinning" with no real progress toward healing.*

I believe we are vulnerable to falling into these emotional pits when we are facing the enemy we know as regret. When we believe our own suboptimal decisions and missteps have been the cause of our setbacks, failures, or painful experiences, these can be the most difficult offenses to forgive. We act as our own judge and jury, passing our own sentence of guilt and shame and condemning our future to self-imposed limitations. Why limitations? Because regret acts as a leash, keeping us from freely moving away from the real or perceived failure. The energy we spend rehearsing poor decisions we've made causes us to be unproductive. Instead, the mistakes we've made should act as fuel for constant growth and learning, propelling us toward our destiny.

Similarly, when we face a crisis (or the negative consequence of someone else's negligence or hurtful actions), we often delay processing our pain because we're laser-focused on ensuring that the individual, community, or system will be held accountable. Whether we are forced to endure pain from a direct, intentional hit or as the collateral damage of another's recklessness, one thing is certain—we cannot, no, we *must* not get stuck in that place of hurt, grief, and, bitterness. Living each day with this bitterness in our hearts will hinder us from moving forward and living our best lives.

The Power of Perspective

What next step should we take to avoid living in replay, regret, or resentment? I believe the answer lives beyond the borders of our painful experiences. We can best package the pain we've identified and prepare it for processing by placing it in proper perspective. We can do this only if we have some means of comparison, some measure of analysis to weigh our discomfort and heartache against. We can begin by looking at those around us—on our street, at our job, in our school, in our church, in our circle of friends, even in our home. When we do, we will find out that *our journey through pain, although real, is not unrivaled or unique to us.*

I don't say this to minimize painful experiences. I'm also not suggesting that we dismiss our hurt and suffering by comparing our ordeals with the misfortunes of others in our communities or the world at large (i.e., "it could always be worse!"). I know I have been guilty of this—as though my brokenness is not worthy of attention because it does not seem to measure up against someone else's on the other side of the globe or the other side of town. In this light, some people believe their problems are too "small" or insignificant to warrant concern, whether that concern comes from a friend, family member, spouse, or spiritual leader. Meanwhile, they continue to bleed, continue to hurt, and continue to carry around their pain and broken pieces without making real progress toward true healing and recovery. As we established in the last chapter, this is not the way.

However, it is important to acknowledge that our "less than best" experiences—yes, even the worst of them—are *shared experiences.* In other words, many of the people we encounter in our lives can identify with what we are facing in that moment. The writer of Ecclesiastes says, "what has been will be again, what has been done will be done again, there is nothing new under the sun" (Ecclesiastes 1:9 New International Version).

Although this verse taken in context is illustrating the cyclical nature of human life, it also implies that our experiences, both good and bad, are not unique to us. Yes, we must acknowledge our pain as being very real with a deeply personal impact on us. However, there is a great deal of *comfort* and life-affirming *perspective* to be found when we can appreciate the commonality of adverse human experiences. As we are hurting, there are many others around us who are hurting too. If we can learn to take a moment to turn our attention to those we work with, live with, and spend our time with, we will discover that most have just overcome some great hurt or are living through a challenging time.

A great illustration of this point is the devastation a natural disaster such as a hurricane can bring. We've all seen emotionally stirring photos and news coverage of the aftermath of a serious hurricane once it's made landfall and wreaked its havoc on cities, communities, and countless lives. Imagine those people stepping out of the evacuation shelter or returning home after the tumultuous winds have ceased and the floodwaters have begun to recede. Surrounded by destruction and debris, the survivors are left to take inventory of what property, possessions, and cherished memorabilia the brutal storm spared, if any.

I cannot imagine how many tears are shed in these moments as the helplessness and hopelessness overwhelms so many hearts and souls. Then after the initial shock, people begin to look up from their individual calamity and see the suffering of others around them. The pain of loss becomes a *shared* experience and a burden that is easier to bear. What happens? A *shift in perspective*. People start helping people; neighbors start helping neighbors. The pain of loss and trauma is real, but the act of people band-ing together in the recovery effort with new perspective provides a healing comfort.

Are You an Extrovert or Introvert?

Your personality type may determine how well you navigate the next step of the journey to healing. Now if you naturally have a more *extroverted* personality—you are someone who tends to *look out into the world* and is *reenergized by those around you*— this second step will come more naturally to you. Seeking comfort and perspective from other people in your circle during the difficult times is instinctive for you. However, if you're like me and lean toward being an *introvert*—meaning you *tend to focus inward* and often *need to retreat* from the world to sort through your emo-tions, regroup, and reboot—this can be challenging. What's worse, if this step is missed, you can feel alone in troubled times, becoming so consumed by painful emotions that it becomes increasingly difficult to see a way out.

As I shared in the last chapter, I know what it feels like to be led by isolation down a troubling, dark path toward hopelessness and depression. Thankfully, I eventually found my way to this next step and was able reach out to others I could trust. This led to two important discoveries on this journey.

The first lesson I learned, stumbling around in the dark, was simple but liberating. I found that as I opened up to those I trusted most about the personal and professional defeat, disappointment, and embarrassment I had been harboring, I became more and more comfortable with shar-ing my story, which opened me up to receive more healing comfort I needed from others. Even though I had been a strong advocate for the emotional health of my patients and my closest friends for years, it felt strange and foreign for me to rely on others for the same. When I chose to shift some energy away from caring for my wounds in solitude and include others in this part of my journey, I was able to pull out of my emotional nosedive and move in a better direction.

The second discovery I made came from listening to similar stories of pain and overcoming from those I now freely confided in. I began to see that the pain I had been drowning in was not unique to *me*. Perhaps I had found myself in my mid-thirties hanging onto a common thread (for dear life!) that binds us all under the sun. The common thread that sometimes falls apart without warning. The common thread of crisis that shows up without any clear, discernable cause or reason. Even the common thread of experiencing failures when we believe we are set up for certain victory. Until this point, I was naïve to this side of the valley. It's not that I had been living an unblemished life without setbacks, disappointments, or the consequences of mistakes. Certainly not! I knew well that life would be full of challenges, whether expected or otherwise. However, I hadn't truly felt the horrible sting of facing defeat after defeat until I was left with a handful of broken dreams, wondering if I would ever recover. In the tales of turmoil, tragedy, and triumph told from the point of view of those who surrounded and supported me, I found the encouragement and perspective I needed to get back up and set out for my win!

Survivors Are All Around You!

Looking back, there were three major groups of people in my life that were positioned just right to be the wells I would draw from on this seemingly dismal and lonely part of my life's journey. The first was my parents. From childhood through the young adult years, my mother committed herself to laying the firm spiritual foundation I would need more than ever in those dark times to come later in life. Beginning in my early college years, my dad stepped into a new role in my young adulthood as a great confidant and advisor. This continued through the tough times of pushing through the rigorous demands of medical schooling through residency and proved to be invaluable when, as they say, life got real—too real—as time went on. In the time of crisis, he seemed to add the right amount of calm, perspective, and reassurance to my seemingly weakening resolve, telling his tales of victory, defeat, second chances, and comebacks.

Next, the support I found in my closest friends was like discovering hidden treasure that was buried in my backyard all along. I cannot emphasize enough how important it is for each of us to take inventory of those we call our friends and associates. With so many of us getting swept up in the age of social media, followers, and virtual relationships, it's easy to lose the value of true camaraderie. The nucleus of friends we keep close during the course of our lives, whether it shrinks or grows with time, will determine not only *how far we can reach* forward to destiny but also *how fast we can recover* from battles we must fight along the way. I can't boast as some do of having a myriad of friends, but I can say that the friendships that I do share have lasted decades, have been fireproofed, and have been lifesaving when it felt as though the walls were caving in on me. Make sure that you can say the same.

While I was hurting, my dearest friends gave me perspective. While I was in a state of depression and disillusionment, they offered conversation, empathy, and the priceless gift of laughter. They constantly reminded me of who I really was (a high-octane, well-educated, goal-oriented achiever!), and they reminded me that I was not alone regardless of how alone I felt. What's more, I felt their presence, waiting and watching on the sidelines to be the first to witness my recovery. They never seemed to lose faith that I would reemerge even better than before whether I believed that at the time or not.

The third tier of support I found in my most difficult season was the most unexpected of them all. In the time I devoted to promoting women's healthcare working in my specialty as an OB/GYN within our medically underserved community, I met and treated so many amazing women. These incredible women may not have been notable for their professional pursuits or high-level connections, but many of them were serious survivors. Many of these remarkable ladies, young and old, had overcome so many hardships whether it was financial hardship, dysfunctional familial and personal relationships, or abuses of many kinds. I marveled at how resilient some of them were, facing crisis after crisis after crisis over the years I knew them yet never giving up hope. They remained committed to weathering the storms of their physical health and social situations, believing for the better. Like the example I gave of how looking around at the devastation of a hurricane sweeping through a city can give perspective on our own damages and loss, listening to my patients' stories of struggle and survival resonated with me deeply. I found out that whether you have more degrees than a thermometer or were a high school dropout, whether you can boast of a strong financial portfolio or have just enough to scrape by, whether you enjoy notoriety or are just a face in the crowd, there is more that binds us than separates us, especially when it comes to the unexpected crises life will sometimes deliver.

It takes a great deal of strength to reach out beyond our own pain while we ourselves are hurting terribly. Among the gifts hidden away for us in this dark and difficult phase of our journey are the people around us, offering much needed support and the light of perspective. It is this support and shift in perspective that brings comfort in our pain. This comfort, in turn, can help move us forward toward real healing.

Taking a Closer Look

"God of all healing counsel! He comes alongside us when we go through hard times, and before you know it, he brings us alongside someone else who is going through hard times so that we can be there for that person just as God was there for us."

—II Corinthians 2: 3–4 (Message Translation)

- How has the replay reel of pain, the enemy we know as regret or bitterness, played a role in your life recently?

- If you're going through a painful or uncomfortable time, are you primarily handling things on your own, or are you drawing on the support and experiences of others?

Find Your Win ●

Follow Wisdom's Lead ●

Focus on What You Have Left ●

Face Your Loss

Find a Different Set of Lenses ●

Feel the Pain ●

CHAPTER 3

Face Your Loss
and Count the Cost!

"Our real blessings often appear to us in the shape of pains, losses and disappointments; but let us have patience and we soon shall see them in their proper figures."

—Joseph Addison, Essayist, Poet, Playwright

The journey through painful circumstances often takes a toll on our lives, and heavy dues can be paid in the form of our energy, focus, or even our mental, physical, and emotional health. One of the primary reasons I decided to write this book was to help as many others as I could to minimize these costs by providing a practical guide to navigate through crisis and come out on the other side with enough reserves to survive and even produce a win in their lives. To ensure this, as I said in the last chapter, we *do* have to be intentional. We have to have a strategy. Once we've acknowledged the hurt by allowing ourselves to truly feel it and have found perspective in the midst of devastating times by identifying with others around us, it's time to take the next step on our journey toward healing, do a little more internal work, and identify what has been lost or stripped away from us. This may at first seem like an unnecessary step, especially in those difficult times of grief when we've lost someone we cared for deeply in relationship or in death. The sum total of our loss in these cases, at least on the surface, seems to be the loved one themselves, yet on closer inspection, the depth of our grief may reach beyond the loss of the person. In the case of a divorce or other dis- solved relationship of great significance, it may not be only the loss of a spouse, friend, or significant other that inflicts deep wounds but also the feelings of failure, rejection, and depression. In the case of the death of a loved one, we can even find ourselves wrestling in our hearts with what feels like the loss of our faith and trust in God and perhaps the loss of any hope for a joyful future at all.

Imagine a woman who has found the love of her life only to lose him suddenly after a few wonderful years of marriage. Many years later, she still finds it impossible to move forward from this terrible loss. She suffers from depression and anxiety and spirals down to the point of considering suicide. Why does she still feel so stuck? Grief is real, and the sense of loss never completely goes away when someone special to us passes away. This is understandable. However, we find that the woman from our example was held back from beginning any real recovery because she never confronted *all* that she believed was taken from her. You see, the loss of the physical spouse was not the only cost. The dreams they dreamed together, the goals and victories they had achieved together, and the possibility of growing a family together were all buried with him. To everyone around her, she was a beautiful, young, intelligent, creative, and caring woman, full of potential and unrealized destiny and eligible for a lifetime of happiness and fulfillment. Until she identified how she perceived her losses in death, she could not reclaim her own life. She was trapped in the mental replay of "what should have been and never can be again." The untimely death of her husband was tragic enough. An even greater tragedy would be a joyless and unfulfilled life lived in the perceived death of her dreams. Thankfully, with the help of medical, spiritual, and social support, she recognized what was happening and, over time, was able to break through and begin to dream new dreams.

Counting up the cost of what we've been through can feel like we're adding pain on top of pain, adding insult to injury. This is why this step is often missed or skipped intentionally. It's bad enough to have to deal with the hurt, right? Why should we go back and take account of all the damage, to "quantify" the hurt? The answer is simple: we cannot know *how* to heal if we don't know *what all* we're healing from. What good would it do a victim of a shooting if they showed up to the ER only to be given pain medication and patched up at the site without an assessment of the deeper damage that may have been done along the bullet's path? Here, it's not just the *surface* or *obvious* harm that the medical team must address. Standard protocol is to immediately begin an investigation for *deeper* or *collateral damage* that the victim may have incurred once they have been stabilized.

This is a graphic but vivid example that illustrates how critical it is to acknowledge the pervasive nature of painful experiences. The deep impact that heartbreak, distress, loss, and grief have on our emotional health, physical well-being, spiritual growth, and outlook on life can be profound and should not be underestimated. We must face the reality of what has happened. We then need to reach out for help to stabilize and gain perspective about our predicament. When we have a better handle on the *scope* of our problem, we can focus energy on digging down to the *depth* of impact the pain has had. Sometimes we've been shaken to our core; at other times, it only feels that way. Doing our best to count the cost of what has been lost, sacrificed, or stolen in the process of facing painful situations will help keep us on the path to our best recovery.

Overestimating the Cost

I'm reminded of a woman who struggled with the exaggerated cost of adverse circumstances and disappointment. She was a beautiful, talented woman who appeared to be blessed in every way. She did well for herself with continued advancement in her career, had a large network of friends, and, as far as I was concerned, was an amazing single mother who seemed to have figured out the secret balancing act of being a working mom. I didn't know how deeply unfulfilled she was. She never had the kind of love relationship she had dreamed of. Sure, she had dated some great guys along the way and enjoyed many good years of married life before a serious relationship breakdown and infidelity led to separation and divorce. After the divorce, she fell into depression, feeling as though she had lost the thing she desired the most: true love and companionship. The problem with this was that she had not yet faced a difficult truth. She had married the "perfect choice" as far as her family was concerned. The marriage she had stayed committed to for two decades never provided her with the intimacy and partnership she needed most. The divorce that he initiated left her feeling empty and alone, but it turned out to be a gift of freedom to find the love she truly desired. By overestimating the cost of the divorce, she created a lonely existence for herself for many years. The void she felt was never created by the divorce. It was still waiting to be filled. She had the opportunity for a second chance at destiny but almost missed it by overestimating the cost of her divorce.

Underestimating the Cost

On the other hand, it is important to avoid underestimating the full impact that crises, setbacks, and even the smallest of hurts can have on our total person—mind, body, and soul. Remember our example of the collateral damage produced by small bullets? The life-threatening injuries are generally beneath the surface. Likewise, a seemingly small offense— hurtful words spoken by a spouse, friend, parent, or colleague, for example—can penetrate quite deeply and create divides that alter our relationships. The injured party feels like they shouldn't feel as bad as they do over something "so small." They make a silent plan to shrug it off and keep moving, yet the offense remains, like a small bullet, moving along and severing positive thoughts, feelings, and attitudes toward the other person.

When we do not assess how we feel in these situations, we actually help forge the path for the bullet of offense to do awful work in our hearts and relationships. The reality is that hurt is hurt. Pain is pain. Tears are tears. It doesn't matter how insignificant the misdeed or hurtful words may seem. We can't allow pride or the fear of being vulnerable to cause us to deny how much we're hurting or how much we've lost in the conflict. Underestimating the cost in this way threatens our peace and even our relationships in the end.

Time to Hang a New Frame

Here's the best news about the important step of taking inventory of the damage incurred from distress or disaster: This is the point at which we can begin the transition from victim to victory. It would seem that having to face the fallout from a failed relationship or dream would create more sadness or hopelessness. On the contrary, with the proper perspective, this phase of the journey does not have to be depressing. This becomes our opportunity to reframe our lives even while our vision is blurred from the tears welling in our eyes. The process of recovery is just that—a *process*. Many of us feel as though we need to wait to feel better before we can decide to look ahead to brighter days. However, while we are still collecting the broken pieces of our hearts, expectations, or carefully constructed plans, we can begin collecting ourselves as well. We can think differently about our seemingly impossible situation.

Let me give you an illustration from my own life. As physicians and surgeons, one of the most feared scenarios of our professional career is carrying the weight of blame of medical error and the lawsuit likely to follow. I did not escape this and had to face litigation relatively early in my career. Although there were several clearly negligent practitioners in the chain of the care of this particular patient prior to my involvement, as the primary surgeon and final link in the chain, I was left to fend for myself in the legal process. On the outside, I appeared fearless and confident in the decisions I had made in caring for the patient. In reality, I was terrified, left wondering if all the years of grueling education, hard training, delayed gratification, personal sacrifice, and my reputation and livelihood could all be lost.

I had overestimated the cost of losing a "perfect practicing record" and misinterpreted the purpose of this storm. It had not come to destroy me or negate the years invested in this career. In the midst of depositions, court appearances, conferences, and board reviews, I had to face the lonely place of pain this conflict produced (remember step 1!). Over time, I found the courage to confide in other colleagues and tell them what I was going through, only to discover that what I was facing was not unique to me at all (step 2). In fact, I found out my case actually paled in comparison to what many others had experienced during their careers. As the dust settled, I began to see the broken pieces of my spotless practice record as an opportunity to reframe how I viewed my professional life. I developed an increased awareness in my everyday practice, which allowed me to make better decisions with every patient encounter. I learned my profession and title did not define me, and opposition was powerless to destroy my identity and purpose. I also started opening up to potential avenues of creativity and revenue, rejecting the limitations of following just one career path for a lifetime. *My win in the course of a difficult circumstance was found in a new frame.*

Beware the Why!

Remember the example of the woman who almost lost her future to grief? I mentioned that her recovery was severely delayed *in part* because she did not know the importance of counting the cost of her loss.

Another key factor helped move her toward healing from a terrible place of pain. Three letters stood between her and her freedom: **W-H-Y**.

"*Why* did this have to happen?"
"*Why* was he taken from me without warning?"
"*Why* can't I have the love I've dreamed of?"
"*Why me*?!"

The unanswered question of "why" echoed in her heart and thoughts night and day. This left her in a dark and lonely place. The constant "whys" helped turn her grief into depression, and the depression almost stole her will to live.

If you have faced a bad situation that seemed unfair, this probably sounds familiar. I know I can relate to this. Harsh circumstances that spin out beyond our control leave us grasping for any hope of understanding the "whys." This is a normal, human response to uncertainty. The real pitfall of asking the "why" questions, however, is that we're left feeling helpless and powerless when there is no reasonable answer to be found. I'm not saying that asking "why" is never reasonable. There are times following crisis situations when looking back for possible causes can shed light on our circumstances, help us avoid repeating similar mistakes, and give us better discernment for the future. However, pursuing an explanation for our crisis sometimes turns into an exhausting mental and emotional exercise that offers no benefit. Worse yet, this can keep us stuck in a holding pattern and even lead to disillusionment in our faith. If we hope for our best recovery through difficult times that we don't understand, we must choose to look forward and not behind. We can search for answers to the "why" questions through prayer, scripture, and counseling, but there is no guarantee of an explanation. There *is* the guarantee all through scripture of God's unyielding presence and plan to bring us to victory, no matter what.

Are Damages Always Damaging?

I hope I've been able to get the point across as to how vital counting the costs of the painful seasons is to proper healing. I can't emphasize enough how critical this step is in our journey. If we can have the courage to face what we've lost and view these losses in their proper context without spending too much effort searching for the answers to potentially unanswerable questions, our ship can make that difficult turn out of the darkness of the storm and steer toward the light of peace, resolution, and victory.

Here's something else to consider. Unless we work in the legal system, we likely don't think about how the word *damages* has opposing meanings. In one sense, we must consider the damages we have incurred because of some traumatic experience. On the other hand, *damages* is also used to describe the *compensation*, the *recompense*, the *payback*, if you will, awarded for losses or injury. What an awesome revelation! If we can find our way through the hurt, even having incurred some damages, we can still come out on the other side with a win—better, stronger, wiser, and well compensated!

I believe when we place our damages in God's hands and learn to be intentional on our journey to healing, we can maximize our retribution and reward. It's my prayer that this guide helps many of you to do just that! For many others, there may be the real need to seek professional help. If that's you, let this book be a beacon of light that illuminates this need and provides you with tools you can use in pursuit of your best healing.

Taking a Closer Look

> *"I consider that our present sufferings are not worth comparing with the glory that will be revealed in us." Romans 8:18 (New International Version)*

- Have you thought about taking an honest inventory of what a painful moment, disappointment, or crisis has cost you? If so, how can you reframe how you think about the impact on your life?

- What "why" questions may be holding you back from moving forward in one or more areas of life?

Find Your Win ●

Follow Wisdom's Lead ●

Focus on What You Have Left

Face Your Loss ●

Find a Different Set of Lenses ●

Feel the Pain ●

CHAPTER 4

Focus on What You Have Left
There's More There Than You Know

*"Every adversity, every failure, and every heart-
ache carries with it the seed of an equivalent or
a greater benefit."*

—Napoleon Hill

Once we've moved through the previous phase and put the
costs of our pain in proper perspective, we should begin
to feel some light moving in, no matter how modest. Every
major victory is a sum total of lesser battles won. This is
especially true when it comes to our mental and emotional
well-being. We should not view any breakthrough as insignificant, even if we find ourselves struggling to get through
the day or we're still crying ourselves to sleep at night. I
say it over and again in this guidebook: working through
particularly painful circumstances is a *process*. There is no
such thing as an overnight success on this journey. You are
probably familiar with the passage "weeping may last for a
night, but joy comes in the morning," adapted from the writ-
ings of the biblical king and psalmist David (see Psalms 30:5,

Amplified Translation). I wholeheartedly believe this to be true, but what happens in the time between the tears and the joy? Life has taught me that *process* lives in this space. It is also the space where our *complete and proper healing* can begin.

We must be cautious not to skip this next key step on our journey, even if we're not sure where to start. (That will usually be true, at least at first, so don't get discouraged!) When we're ready, it's time to take a different kind of inventory—one that doesn't tally our losses but looks at what we have left! No matter how drained or defeated we may feel by a painful situation, *we always have something left.* Further, *what we have left is more than enough to pull us through the storm to a safe haven of recovery and victory.* It doesn't matter what's been lost—a job or career, a financial investment, a position, a dream, a relationship, or even a loved one—our entire life's reserves have *never* been depleted. *Ever.* I admit it often does not feel that way, especially when we've lost more than one thing we hold valuable at nearly the same time.

A good friend of mine had to truly battle her way through this step in her journey. Since high school, I knew her to be a bright, ambitious person. She was more introverted than most of the people I've grown close to over the years, but she was no one's doormat. She was clear about what she wanted out of life and had her own voice—she just didn't feel she had to yell over everyone else to be heard. I watched her thrive in advanced placement classes in high school and in her nursing program in college. After graduation, we went our separate ways to conquer our own places of the world. We kept in touch over the next ten or fifteen years, although not as much as either of us would have liked.

I assumed that like me, her years were being spent busying about, striving for her dreams and her best life. I did not know that an abusive and controlling spouse had been craftily derailing her dreams and silencing her voice altogether.

When she opened up to me about what had been going on, I was devastated and determined to help her find her voice again in any way I could. The key was for her to see for herself that just as she had given her power away to her spouse, she could take it back! She had been stuck at step three for years. She could identify all that had been lost—happiness, self-esteem, security, financial independence, and many years of experience and development in her career—but she needed to discover what she had left! *Practically speaking, she had a few supportive family members a few states away, close friends in her corner willing to see her through, and an active nursing license awaiting renewal!* With these tools and a revived will for a better life for herself and her children, she was able to break free from that toxic relationship, relocate closer to her family and support system, rebuild her career, and forge a new path toward wholeness.

What's in Your Wreckage?

Following the hurricanes that wreak havoc in our lives, what remains can be used to rebuild for the next season. It is not easy to let go of what has been lost, but we ought not choose to stay stuck, lamenting things and relationships that have been lost. In looking back for too long, we miss opportunities to gather what we need to move forward toward proper healing. It took me far too long to get to this fourth phase of recovery following my unexpected second divorce. The personal loss and public failure felt far too great to recover from. The dream of taking my happiness, family, and ministry to that next level of my destiny seemed to have washed away in an instant without warning. I couldn't figure out what I had done to deserve such life-altering disappointment. It felt like just as I was setting sail out to sea on this triumphant journey as a witness of redemption, the ship veered toward the rocks and was demolished. I could see only the wreckage surrounding me, and I almost drowned in those shallow waters.

An important turning point came when I saw how the years were passing and I was still standing in the same place. This was an interesting revelation that held double meaning. I was making little progress toward my own healing and yet was being preserved where I was. I realized that the darkness had never consumed me, though I was certain more times than I could count that it would. I was still standing. I was somehow thriving in my career, raising a child without a guidebook for emotionally distraught divorced moms, and helping others in my sphere of influence reach for higher plains in their own lives. How could this be? *The answer was hidden in the wreckage in plain sight.* I had what I needed to move forward in my hands all along. I possessed the forgiveness I needed to release others and even to release myself for falling short. I possessed the "dream maker" in my heart that needed a reboot so that I could allow myself to dream new dreams—set new markers for happiness and fulfillment. I clearly possessed the strength to pull myself up out of this place and start moving forward. After all, I was still standing!

Let It Burn!

Having lived in various parts of the Midwest before moving to Southern California, I'm as comfortable surrounded by farmlands or dense forestry as I am sandy beaches and palm trees. Growing up, I found the practice of *controlled burning*, often used in farming and forest management, interesting. As city and suburb dwellers, when we hear the word *fire*, we think of something that presents danger to people and destruction of our infrastructure. However, in agriculture and forestry, fires are often intentionally set in a controlled manner to clear weeds, encourage growth of the most desirable trees and plants, and expose a layer of soil beneath that will be even more productive in renewing the land. *Fire in this context is used to reveal what is needed for future success*—that is, once the flames die down and the smoke clears.

Similarly, when we are learning to master the process of moving through painful experiences, we learn to search for the treasure and tools in the ashes of what we've lost. What remains will enable us to pick up and move forward. What lies beneath the surface of our trauma? There is often a strength and resilience we didn't know we possessed. We find out we have resources and abilities that we never tapped into. We uncover fresh dreams and visions that we may not have thought to chase before or that we kept on the back burner while we continued in our usual routines. This is an interesting time of potentially great discovery and creativity but only if we can find a way to tap into it even while we feel powerless and uninspired.

You may be familiar with the inspirational story of the notable author Joanne Rowling, better known by her pen name J. K. Rowling. I have drawn encouragement from her personal story for many years, and it is fitting to tell it at this stage of our journey. Rowling is best known for her creation of a wildly popular children's fantasy book series that became a global phenomenon. Though now she is one of the world's wealthiest women, she birthed a literary empire in times of pure hardship and crisis. Having survived the death of her mother, a short-lived, tumultuous marriage, single parenting in poverty, depression, and plenty of rejection, all at a fairly young age, she emerged from the ashes an incredible success using only what she had left—her imagination and skill as a writer. What an amazing lesson! There is so much to uncover after crisis, perhaps even enough to build an empire, if we know to look for what is left.

A Time for Gratitude

Focusing on what we have left, an opportunity opens for us to consider how thankful we are for all that was never touched by the storm that blew into our lives. In the case of a physical storm or accident, this may be gratefulness that our lives have been spared. In the case of a bitter divorce, this may be gratefulness that our sanity is intact! In the case of a financial crisis, this may be gratefulness for the supportive people and valuable relationships that we have maintained. Whatever has not become collateral damage or directly impacted by the trauma is eligible for our gratitude. On some of the darker days in my life, the smile or boisterous laugh of my child allowed me to tap into the vein of gratefulness.

"Do not be anxious about anything, but in every situation, by prayer and petition, ***with thanksgiving***, present your requests to God. And the ***peace of God***, which transcends all understanding ***will guard your hearts and your minds*** in Christ Jesus." Philippians 4:6–7 (New International Version)

The shift toward gratitude, even for a moment, allows the peace we need to move in and settle our hearts so that we can focus on what step to take next. Gratitude provides the light we need to illuminate our path out of the valley. We often spend far too much time on step three of our journey, taking inventory of what we've lost. It is quite difficult to rebuild our broken lives while we're weighted down with a spirit of defeat.

We need to refocus our energy toward gratefulness for what we have left. Finding our way to thankfulness is an important key to getting the win we need when all hell has decided to break out. With what we find among the wreckage, we can build again, and with our grateful heart, we can harness the energy we need to do it.

Taking a Closer Look

> "*We **are hard pressed on every side, but not crushed**; perplexed, but not in despair; persecuted, but not abandoned; **struck down but not destroyed**." II Corinthians 4:8–9 (New International Version)*

- After taking an inventory of what was lost during a painful experience, what tools/skills/support persons/dreams/passions were left to help you recover? Did you recognize them at the time?

- Do you find it difficult to tap into gratefulness when you're going through a difficult season? (I know I do!) What simple things can you do to turn on the thankfulness at this phase of the journey?

Find Your Win ●

Follow Wisdom's Lead

Focus on What You Have Left ●

Face Your Loss ●

Find a Different Set of Lenses ●

Feel the Pain ●

CHAPTER 5

Follow Wisdom's Lead
Rebuild or Start Anew?

*"It's not what they take away from you that
counts. It's what you do with what you have left."*

—Hubert H. Humphrey, American politician,
38th Vice President of the United States, Lead
Author of the Civil Rights Act of 1964

I hope that so far you have found this guide helpful, whether you find yourself navigating your way through a recent crisis or equipping yourself for the next challenging circumstance you'll meet. I know one thing for sure—trying times are sure to come, no matter who we are or where we find ourselves. That's a fact of life. How we meet these challenges makes all the difference.

I find this next phase of our journey the most interesting. Why do I say this? Well, it is here where we find ourselves standing between the chaos and turmoil behind us and our healing and victory ahead of us. We have only one important question to ask and answer—"what's next?"

You've survived confronting your pain head on, you've gained some perspective on your situation, and you've taken account of what was lost during a difficult time. Now armed with what you have left, the crisis brings you to a crossroads. If you want to avoid getting stuck in this valley, you have to now be intentional and strategize. Which path do you take? Do you rebuild, or do you start anew?

This may seem intuitive, but I guarantee you that for many people struggling through painful scenarios, the answer to these questions may not be clear. The sadness, disappointment, or unforgiveness that remain cloud our judgment and make it difficult to make optimal decisions. It happens to the best of us. This can be a vulnerable time, and we are not always operating at our best. We don't recognize how much energy, focus, and strength have been diverted toward surviving the storm and keeping our heads above water. With the shoreline in sight, we have to recharge and refocus our attention to problem solving and decision making.

There are times when it is clear what to do next, especially if it appears the next decision to be made has already been made for us. When we're devastated by the loss of a loved one, for example, the truth is that we have only one choice on this part of our journey—we must find a way to move forward without their physical presence in our lives. We carry all of our love for the departed, our most cherished memories, and even the empty space their absence has left in our heart into our next moments, and this makes every day that we choose to live a life of purpose a victory.

There are other times when the decision to rebuild what we've lost or to start anew may not be clear. We may have to sift through a host of pros and cons, or we may have to lean on the wisdom and experiences of others to determine which path to take. As a practical example, when a family's home is destroyed by a wildfire, mudslide, or earthquake, rebuilding the home may be considered too great a risk, but starting anew may cause the family members to be uprooted from the community, schools, church, and support they value. They have to ask, "Does the risk of staying here outweigh the benefits? Are we better off starting over somewhere else?"

As if this isn't challenging enough, pain has a habit of blending what would ordinarily be black-and-white situations into nebulous shades of gray. Confusion, uncertainty, and anxiety are the enemies of clarity when we are faced with making critical life decisions. It's vital to our healing that we give special attention to a few important concerns when deciding whether to rebuild or start anew. There are some key concepts we cannot afford to ignore at this phase of our journey. If we do, we run the risk of carrying too much dysfunction with us, diminishing our true win, or stalling out altogether. I introduce to you the three "Fs"— forgiveness, fundamental life lessons, and faith reservoir.

Forgiveness

This is a tough topic to address, but forgiveness may hold the key to much of what happens at this stage. This includes forgiving others and/or forgiving ourselves. In chapter two, we addressed dealing with regret and bitterness. Most of us understand what forgiveness *really* is. It's releasing someone else, or ourselves, from the sentence deserved for hurting us or for severely falling short. We exchange vengeance and punishment for mercy and compassion. However, it's just as important to recognize what forgiveness is *not*. While we're working through the emotions we're feeling and trying to choose the best path, we need to remember that forgiveness is *not* excusing or justifying destructive behavior nor does it imply reconciliation. A perfect example is a marriage and family fractured by infidelity. The couple will have to decide whether to rebuild the broken relationship or divorce and start anew. Without forgiveness, neither decision will lead to an optical outcome—reconciliation or healthy co-parenting. The root of bitterness and resentment will contaminate and sabotage either arrangement.

What about those times when we believe we are the primary cause of our own unhappiness? Over the years, I have found that forgiving myself can be much harder than forgiving someone else. Facing *both the perpetrator and victim* in the mirror every day can seem unbearable. Like many people my age, I have been around long enough to make foolish mistakes that have cost me time, money, relationships, and several nights' sleep. "How could I be so stupid?" "How could I have been so careless?" "How could I have missed all of those red flags?" Any of that sound familiar? I'm sure it does! Looking back over my life, sometimes it's hard to believe that my life script includes two divorces, single parenting, and major financial mistakes. I have to remind myself that my life script also includes great fortitude and courage, academic and professional success, and a strong spiritual center that has been shaken but never crushed!

To forgive ourselves for making downright bad decisions, we can begin by giving ourselves more grace. In many cases we are not being fair to ourselves, as we may have made many of these so-called "bad" decisions working within the framework of our own limited life experience, information, and perspective. It's true that we cannot go back in time and undo what has been done, but we *can* do much better going forward. Our failures are often are our best teachers.

Fundamental Life Lessons

Along those lines, the next "F," fundamental life lessons, comes into play. This is the time to ask ourselves, "Are there any important life lessons that I need to take away from this experience?" This isn't the first time you're hearing this, but the implications here are huge. We can't afford to miss or overlook what we should learn while deciding if we should continue with what remains of our own investments—whether this involves money, time, or relationship—or walk away and start fresh. The lessons we're being taught in painful times can provide insight on which way to go and equip us with wisdom and discernment we can use to our advantage going forward.

When a small business fails, many factors play into the next steps the owner will take. Whether to rebuild and reinvest in the dream or walk away and take a different avenue will be largely determined by financial factors. Lessons learned about other areas relevant to the business, including product, location, marketing strategies, and partnerships, should also factor into which path to take. If these lessons learned are taken into account, any future business venture will be created not just by a dreamer or visionary but by an informed and battle-tested entrepreneur armed for better success.

Faith Reservoir

As we are finding our way out of the dark valley of a painful season and choosing which path to take, what remains in our faith reservoir may be the greatest determiner of the magnitude of our victory. The purpose of this guide is to aide us in securing a real life win and minimize our own personal dysfunction as we navigate through challenging circumstances. Much like the "brightness" control function on our television remotes, smartphones, and tablets, *our faith and expectation will tend to control the light in our lives.* We need to have a sufficient amount of faith and hopeful expectation to fuel our next move.

Opposition, trauma, and the disappointment of this painful season can dim the brightness of our hope for the next season to come. It is important to take a real, honest look at where we are especially when we come from a strong religious background or have come to believe our greatest value as a person lies in our inexhaustible strength and stability. *Pressures and harsh life circumstances can appear to threaten our outlook and challenge our faith.* I learned this tough truth in my mid-thirties. Make sure at this phase that you know the status of your faith reservoir. Ask yourself, "Have I lowered my expectations in life as a result of this last hit?" If you discover that your faith reservoir is running dangerously low, replace what has been drained before deciding whether to rebuild or pick up and start over.

I don't have a universal formula to help restore failing faith. I wish I did. What I can share is what has helped me in those difficult times. Watching, reading, and listening to biographies of the "greats" is so encouraging when I need to boost my engines and brighten my outlook. I am reminded that uncommon champions such as Nelson Mandela, Winston Churchill, Rosa Parks, and Steve Jobs were all imperfect people like you and me who possessed the uncanny ability to convert major life setbacks into springboards that would catapult them to the next chapter of their destiny. I use their examples of recovery to refuel my faith in what is possible for my future, no matter how dismal things seem at the time.

Likewise, I surround myself with people and conversations that are uplifting and encouraging. People in my life who I adore but have a tendency toward "glass half-empty" thinking are kept at bay. I intentionally read books and listen exclusively to sermons and lectures that are all geared toward building faith and hopeful expectation for the future.

Most important of all, I employ a combination of prayer, life-affirming scripture, and destiny-building declarations to refill my reservoir. Generally, what I'm praying and declaring is contrary to what I'm seeing or feeling at first. With time, and without fail, what I feel begins to align with what I say and, ultimately, what I say becomes what I believe. Thus, my tank fills up once more!

There is a lot in this short chapter to digest, but we are making another major turning point in our journey. Although we are often feeling a bit weary at this point, we're also positioning ourselves to emerge from those darker valleys and move to higher ground. Whether we decide to put our energy toward rebuilding at the wreckage site or relocate and start anew, *we are ready to emerge.* We are approaching a place of victory.

Taking a Closer Look

*"Forget the former things; do not dwell on the past.
See, I am doing a new thing! Now it springs up;
do you not perceive it? I am making a way in the
wilderness and streams in the wasteland." Isaiah
43: 18–19 (New International Version)*

*"Blessed are those who find wisdom, those who
gain understanding." Proverbs 3:13 (New International Version)*

At this phase of our journey, we decide what to do next—
rebuild or start over? Here are some points to consider in
making that decision.

- Is this a dream, goal, or relationship worth
  saving? How much do I have invested?

- What red flags are waving that I cannot afford to
  ignore while trying to make this critical decision?

- Have new dreams, ideas, and options been con-
  ceived from this situation?

- Do I have any bitterness in my heart that I need to address before I move forward?

- What is the reading on my "faith reservoir" tank? Do I need to fill up? What steps can I take to refill my tank?

Find Your Win

Follow Wisdom's Lead

Focus on What You Have Left

Face Your Loss

Find a Different Set of Lenses

Feel the Pain

CHAPTER 6

Find Your Win
and Celebrate Your Survival!

*"Remember to celebrate milestones as you pre-
pare for the road ahead."*

—Nelson Mandela, Activist, Philanthropist,
Former President of South Africa

If you've stayed the course with this guide, I am confident
that you have come a long way on this journey. Everyone
experiences pain in life. The circumstances may differ and
the reaction to those circumstances vary from person to
person, but no one is exempt from the sting of disappointment, terrible hurt, or loss.

Through my own pain, I've made some important discoveries and am blessed to have shared them with you. It is
my hope that you have been able to embrace the importance
of facing your pain head-on and learn to reach beyond
yourself in some way in those dark times. You are not alone
in your storm. It has been my goal to show you why it is so
necessary to take a real inventory of all that has been lost
or damaged and to appreciate all that has been spared to

aid in your recovery. At this crossroads, you have learned to carefully consider whether it is in the best interest of your purpose and destiny to rebuild or reconsider your life direction.

Before we move on to our final step in this journey, I want to give you a strong word of caution. Even if you follow this guide to the letter or find an alternative path through the darkness to victory over pain, it is important to recognize that you have likely spent a great deal of emotional, mental, and physical energy along the way. This is no small matter. I was not always aware of this fact, and it cost me more than I would like to imagine. Did you know that winning doesn't always feel like we think it should?

When we're down and out, we yearn for the day when our fragmented lives will realign and our joy will return. We keep imagining the warmth on our face once the clouds finally pass and the sun shines again. However, a quiet enemy of our joy and recovery may yet be lurking, and we must be aware of exhaustion. The exhaustion we may feel on our journey from injury to healing has the potential to steal away the celebration of our victory. Bishop T. D. Jakes, renowned preacher, teacher, and author, warns us in one of his many life-changing sermons this way—*don't drown in shallow waters*. What a frightful concept that we can come all this way and lose steam just as we're making our greatest breakthrough to shore in shallow waters!

I encountered a challenging season of hardship and opposition. In one season, I found myself dealing with an abrupt marital separation and divorce, a professional lawsuit, chronic pain from a massive abdominal hernia due to a difficult pregnancy, and the uncommon fatigue that accompanies juggling single parenting a young child and a demanding career. I feel confident that I could have handled one or two of these issues at one time without much trouble. This wasn't the case. I was fighting a major battle on every front all at the same time, without much relief. It didn't take long in this environment for depression to set in, although this went undiagnosed. One thing is for sure—I discovered the awesome combined power of caffeine and prayer for survival!

Over time, and by the grace of God, I found my way through this complicated and distressing time, which ultimately prompted me to write this book. I am grateful for this testimony that I have to share with others. The separation and divorce created an opportunity to work better together as co-parents with the common goal of raising a well-rounded, God-fearing child. The lawsuit resolved within a few years, and my career made an upswing to promotion during the worst of it. The pain from the hernia became unbearable after a couple of years, but it was repaired by an amazingly skilled surgeon who even amazed himself with the outcome! My beautiful daughter thrived while her mother survived, and on the job, my patient care and professionalism never suffered. However, the war was not won when the storms all ceased. After several years of hard-fought battles, I was standing in victory, yet I didn't feel victorious. I didn't feel light, free, or happy. I felt only exhaustion and found myself in shallow waters and in danger of drowning.

The energy I needed to dream new dreams and form an action plan for new goals had been nearly depleted in battle. I was no longer overwhelmed with all of the external troubles or the weight of depression, but I was left with pure fatigue in the aftermath, and that exhaustion seemed to cancel out my joy. Thankfully, this was not the end of the story! It took some effort, but I found a way to pull through, and I want to share with you three secrets that helped me to get safely to shore.

Don't Rehearse the Past

We've all heard that a key to moving forward in life is letting go of the past. How do we go about this? How can we let go of our past when every life experience, good and bad, has gone into shaping the person we've become? Not to mention the power of human memory and the importance of memory in retaining information we need to learn and optimize our future decision making? If you stub your toe on the leg of the living room coffee table hard enough to bring tears to your eyes, although that is one painful memory, it behooves you to store that experience in your memory to avoid doing that again, right?

Likewise, we need to use painful encounters from the past to grow in wisdom, discernment, and character. However, there is a vast difference between *learning from* the past and *rehearsing* the past. Replaying the negative events over and over in our minds like a feature film that's always cued up and ready to go is *extremely* counterproductive. When we should be rejoicing over our survival and recovery, we instead exhaust our energy in rehashing and lamenting. No, we cannot forget the painful things that have happened to us—in fact, the stored memories may be useful in preventing harm down the road. However, it is not wise or productive to constantly replay those painful moments in our thoughts and in our conversation every chance we get. We do not need to engage in this type of self-injury to validate the magnitude of our crises and traumas.

When I started applying this valuable truth to my own life, I can honestly say that much of the heaviness I had been carrying from the past began to lift, giving me more energy and a desire to *want* to celebrate my victories. Over time, I started to identify less and less with the victim in me that had endured hardship and more with the champion in me that was preserved and ready for the next chapter of life.

Rest and Recharge

While we're busy trying to recover and rebound from a major disappointment or grieving the loss of a loved one, life continues to go on around us. What's more, life continues to make its usual demands on us. We do our best to continue in our expected routine and push through daily responsibilities. We're still going to our classes, getting through the work day, looking for a new job, managing the kids, going to church, paying the bills, dealing with the car repairs, and even dragging the garbage and recycling bins out to the curb on time. Whatever it is, we keep doing it. *We try our best to juggle functioning and healing at the same time.*

In the real world, this balancing act cannot be avoided, but we must find ways to recharge. Life won't stop and wait for us to heal, so we have to choose to stop whenever possible. As I've said, the journey through painful times often produces fatigue or exhaustion even when we're positioned to overcome. Without realizing it, we often find ourselves on the other side of crisis operating at a disadvantage we're not accustomed to. We're making day-to-day decisions or major life decisions with mental, emotional, and physical batteries that are dangerously low on power.

Before I went through a seemingly never-ending season of battles and challenges, I equated rest and relaxation with unproductivity and stagnancy. I learned later that this is not true. It is necessary to make rest a priority. For me, this translated into anything from scheduling a massage to enjoying a quiet afternoon at the park and even learning to trust others to care for my daughter while I stayed in bed all Saturday afternoon watching my favorite shows! It doesn't matter what you choose to do to rest and reset. I only recommend that you choose simple pleasures—those things that will not demand much energy and will, instead, add a little strength and joy to your heart. My hope is that these simple gestures of rest and self-care will go a long way in contributing to your victorious recovery in the end.

Celebrate You, and Be Your Own Reward

One mistake we often make is waiting for the storm to fully subside before we acknowledge any victory. That is a time to celebrate your win, but it should not be the *only* time. As I've stressed throughout this practical guide, our journey through pain is *a process*. Pushing forward through painful times of uncertainty and sorrow can feel like a bad drama playing out with no end in sight.

We learned that although we cannot forget painful times from our past, we must find a way to stop replaying these events in our minds and conversations if we are to properly heal. We have also learned that we must find ways to recharge and replenish the energy that is drained from us in a way that only surviving hardship can do. We should take it one step further and become intentional about celebrating every victory along the road to our recovery!

By celebrating each victory, great and small, I mean that *you should give yourself the well-deserved recognition for every positive move you make on this journey toward converting your pain into a new life win.* This could mean a small reward such as a favorite snack or dessert for choosing not to call into work or stay under the covers when your fight feels low. It could be springing for a babysitter and scheduling an afternoon massage or going for afternoon brunch if you're feeling it!

I will never forget the day I sent myself a beautiful bouquet of flowers with a card that read, "No one is more proud of you than me. You will soon have all your heart desires and more! With God all things are possible." Now that may seem silly or frivolous, but I can tell you that having a visible reminder of my survival, progress, and healing sitting beautifully on my dining room table during darker times was priceless. I still keep this card in a drawer as a reminder to this day. It sits in my drawer as a trophy. A prolonged season of hardship could have destroyed me, but it did not. The smaller celebrations—the dinner out, the new pair of shoes, the bouquet of flowers—helped to keep my joy afloat during difficult times. Working together with my faith and my support system, I believe these smaller celebrations translated into greater victories for me over time.

It is wonderful to be surrounded by people who love us and lift us up when we're down. However, there will most certainly be times when you need to encourage yourself—be your own cheerleader to victory. Don't spend all of your energy being your own worst enemy and stewing in regret and self-blame. Let the little acts of celebration and self-encouragement be the rudder that guides your broken ship toward the shore. As the tide begins to turn—and it will, *believe me*—the strongest part of you that you've been rewarding along the way will overshadow the rest. You will emerge as more than a survivor—you will emerge as the victor who turned pain and tragedy into a life win.

Don't forget to celebrate that!

Taking a Closer Look

> *"Don't be afraid, I've redeemed you. I've called your name. You're mine. When you're in over your head, I'll be there with you.* **When you're in rough waters, you will not go down.** *When you're between a rock and a hard place, it won't be a dead end." Isaiah 43:1–4 (Message Translation)*

> *"For* **I know the plans I have for you**,*" declares the Lord, "plans to prosper you and not to harm you,* **plans to give you hope and a future**.*" Jeremiah 29:11 (New International Version)*

> *"But thanks be to God!* **He gives us the victory** *through our Lord Jesus Christ." I Corinthians 15:57 (New International Version)*

- Now that we've come to the end of this journey together, think about your default setting when facing painful moments. Are you prone to staying down and out, weighed down by rehearsing the hurt, or do you find that there is a fight in you to live out your best recovery in celebrating the small daily victories?

- What simple things can you do for yourself that can give you a lift or mark small victories in difficult and challenging times?

- Have you considered sharing your powerful story of overcoming?

CHAPTER 7

The "D" Word
A Brief Commentary on Battling Depression

As much as I wanted to end this guided tour through processing pain on a victorious note, I felt it important to include a note on the notorious "D" word: depression. The importance of this topic cannot be overstated. Although the subject of depression still remains taboo in many homes, communities, and places of worship, recent efforts have been made to raise awareness of this very prevalent and potentially devastating mental health disorder through media and public health campaigns. However, there is still much work to be done.

It's estimated that 15 percent of adults eighteen years or older will experience depression at some point in their life according to data provided by the National Institute of Mental Health. As of 2016, over sixteen million adults age eighteen years or older had experienced an episode of major depression in the previous year, and this is even more common among adolescents. Women are twice as likely as men to experience depression. One out of seven women even suffer postpartum depression, half of whom are having the symptoms during their pregnancy.

Depression affects people from all walks of life regardless of race, education, or socioeconomic status. The worst part is that it's not always recognized by the one suffering or those around them. I have found that one significant barrier to increased self-awareness is the belief some hold that admitting to depression is admitting to weakness, failure, or even insufficient religious faith.

Depression can have a number of potential causes. Family tree (i.e., genetics), alterations in brain chemistry or hormones, poor physical health, and painful life experiences can contribute to an episode or lifetime struggle with depression. Further, the impact depression may have on a person's life is rarely limited in scope. Self-image, work performance, home life, and relationships can all become shrouded in the darkness of depression, leaving little light for *inspiration* or *aspiration*.

It is important to remember that sadness or grief as a result of some painful life experience or crisis can be a normal part of the human experience and are not always evidence of true clinical depression. In fact, sadness, anger, and other similar emotions may be present to draw our attention to broken areas in our life that need to be recognized and healed. We do not want to live a life *controlled* by emotions. Yet, it is equally dangerous to ignore what sadness, anxiety, and pain may be trying to *illuminate*, just as it would be dangerous to ignore flashing warning signs when driving along the road.

Depression is not synonymous with having a really bad day, weathering a period of sadness, or coping with grief related to personal loss (although bereavement and depression have similar symptoms and can be difficult to tell apart). The term *depression* is commonly used to describe a variety of "down" moods and feelings we experience, but it more accurately describes a large group of serious and well-defined clinical disorders. Medically speaking, true clinical depression is a mental health disorder that deeply affects the sufferer's emotional state as well as their overall quality of life and sense of well-being.

Hallmarks of typical clinical depression (also known as major depressive disorder or MDD) include *persistent* sadness, loss of interest in once-enjoyable activities, isolation, fatigue, changes in weight and/or sleep patterns, difficulty concentrating, feelings of guilt and worthlessness, and recurring morbid thoughts of death and suicide. The key is that some or all of these symptoms are present for more than *two weeks*.

Whether the depression is typical, atypical, or chronic, it is important to locate where we (or someone we care about) may be along this spectrum of disorders. We do this by becoming more aware of when things are not right with us or our loved ones. Persistent sadness, apathy, tiredness, "emotional eating," feelings of guilt or worthlessness, withdrawal, and isolation can all be clear signs of depression.

The screening tool called the Patient Health Questionnaire-9 (PHQ-9) is commonly used by healthcare professionals. It helps us better recognize if many of our patient's background thoughts, feelings, and behaviors are evidence of some form of depression.

PATIENT HEALTH QUESTIONNAIRE-9 (PHQ-9)

Over the last 2 weeks, how often have you been bothered by any of the following problems? (Use "✔" to indicate your answer)	Not at all	Several days	More than half the days	Nearly every day
1. Little interest or pleasure in doing things	0	1	2	3
2. Feeling down, depressed, or hopeless	0	1	2	3
3. Trouble falling or staying asleep, or sleeping too much	0	1	2	3
4. Feeling tired or having little energy	0	1	2	3
5. Poor appetite or overeating	0	1	2	3
6. Feeling bad about yourself — or that you are a failure or have let yourself or your family down	0	1	2	3
7. Trouble concentrating on things, such as reading the newspaper or watching television	0	1	2	3
8. Moving or speaking so slowly that other people could have noticed? Or the opposite — being so fidgety or restless that you have been moving around a lot more than usual	0	1	2	3
9. Thoughts that you would be better off dead or of hurting yourself in some way	0	1	2	3

FOR OFFICE CODING ___0___ + _____ + _____ + _____

=Total Score: _____

If you checked off any problems, how difficult have these problems made it for you to do your work, take care of things at home, or get along with other people?

Not difficult at all	Somewhat difficult	Very difficult	Extremely difficult
☐	☐	☐	☐

Developed by Drs. Robert L. Spitzer, Janet B.W. Williams, Kurt Kroenke and colleagues, with an educational grant from Pfizer Inc. No permission required to reproduce, translate, display or distribute.

Based on this simple survey, answered honestly, it is possible to identify if someone is dealing with depression and the degree of severity. The key is to *answer honestly*. If there is any concern that depression may have you or a loved one in its grip, *you need to seek help*. Support and treatment for depression of all forms are *readily available*. Depression hotlines, therapists, healthcare providers, church counselors, and even your most trusted friend or family members are great places to start. Management can range from modifications in diet and activity to incorporating natural supplements, intensive therapy, and medication. Just as life experiences and genetic makeup vary, so does the manner in which we experience depression. One size does *not* fit all. Teaming up with a professional gives us the power to do battle with this serious disease using the weapons and tools that will be most effective.

Christianity and Depression—A Contradiction?

Here's a very interesting question—can a Christian be depressed? An even better question is if a Christian is suffering from depression, does that negate their faith? *Absolutely not!* Let me repeat that—*absolutely not!* Would we ask the same about someone who is ill from exposure to a flu virus, diabetes, or cancer? Of course not! A long-held misbelief in churches of many denominations is that mental health disorders (depression, anxiety, bipolar disorder) are *solely* spiritual matters and should be dealt with *solely* by spiritual means. There is a *very real* need and application for prayer and scripture in addressing depression. However, mental health disorders should be addressed with as much care and attention as any serious physical ailment. A woman recently diagnosed with breast cancer would be encouraged to add specialized oncology care, chemotherapy, radiation, dietary changes, and regular group support sessions to her faith, prayer, and bible study. Likewise, depression is a serious and potentially life-threatening disorder that should be managed with a holistic approach.

Admitting that we are engaged in a battle for our mental health and well-being is not a failure of faith or fortitude. In fact, it takes a great deal of strength to confront the depression that leaves us feeling hopeless and powerless. It takes a great deal of courage to come out from behind our smiling facade and ask for help. Many of us are so used to receiving praise for "holding it together" that it seems uncharacteristic for us to face a giant that is not so easily slain. I know about this firsthand.

Admitting that we may be suffering from depression does not diminish the champion within us. Being honest with ourselves and seeking the help we need ensures that the champion our family, our children, our friends, our coworkers, and our patients look to can live to fight another day! If we are suffering from depression, we *can* face it, and *we should not face it alone.* The support, therapy, behavior and lifestyle modification recommendations, and sometimes the life-saving medication we may need are all within reach.

If you need help, you are one decision away from finding your way to peace and wholeness. Please make that decision *today.*

If you're not sure where to start, these resources are available twenty-four hours a day, seven days a week to help.

- Mental Healthline at 1-833-864-3525 can connect you to individualized mental health recovery and treatment options (mentalhealthline.org).

- If you or someone you know may be experiencing symptoms of postpartum depression, education and resources are available at 1800ppdmoms.org.

- The National Suicide Prevention Lifeline at 1-800-273-TALK (8255) immediately connects you to the nearest crisis center for intervention, support, education, and helpful resources (a lifeline chat feature is also available at SuicidePreventionLifeline.org).

- Online counseling services with trained personnel via chat, video, and phone are available at betterhelp.com.

9 781643 881294